TRUDEAU'S DARKEST HOUR

TRUDEAU'S DARKEST HOUR

War Measures in Time of Peace

October 1970

Edited by

Guy Bouthillier and Édouard Cloutier

Baraka
Books

Library and Archives Canada Cataloguing in Publication

Trudeau's darkest hour; War Measures in time of peace, October 1970 / Guy Bouthillier, Édouard Cloutier.

Includes bibliographical references.

ISBN 978-1-926824-04-8

1. Québec (Province)—History—October Crisis, 1970. 2. Civil rights—Québec (Province). I. Bouthillier, Guy, 1939- II. Cloutier, Edouard

FC2925.9.025T79 2010   971.4'04   C2010-904796-6

Cover by Folio infographie
Photo Montreal La Presse/Canadian Press
Book design by Folio infographie

Legal Deposit, 3rd quarter, 2010
Bibliothèque et Archives nationales du Québec
Library and Archives Canada

Published by Baraka Books of Montreal.
6977, rue Lacroix
Montréal, Québec H4E 2V4
Telephone: 514-808-8504
info@barakabooks.com
www.barakabooks.com

Printed and bound in Quebec

Trade Distribution & Returns
Canada
LitDistCo
1-800-591-6250; orders@litdistco.ca

United States
Independent Publishers Group
1-800-888-4741 (IPG1); orders@ipgbook.com

To the memory of Tommy Douglas.
"He showed political courage of the highest order."

CONTENTS

INTRODUCTION

The war measures were invoked formally in response to the kidnapping of British trade commissioner James Cross on October 5 and Quebec Labour minister Pierre Laporte on October 10. Canada was faced with two serious "political" crimes, however they had not simply appeared out of nowhere. Other countries faced even greater turmoil. May '68 had literally shaken the foundations of France, while the long hot summers in the 1960s in the United States, combined with spectacular political assassinations—John F. and Robert Kennedy, Malcolm X, and Martin Luther King Jr.—left scars on that country that continue to fester. On May 4, 1970, the United States National Guard opened fire on a demonstration at Ohio's Kent State University and left four students dead. All this happened in the run-up to Canada's crisis in 1970 and the people of Canada were fully aware of these events that were taking place in other countries. Similarly, the federal government, the RCMP, and even the Canada's military had been closely monitoring political activism in Canada ever since FLQ set off its first bombs 1963. Dan Loomis, Reg Whitaker, and Desmond Morton make this very clear in this book. Two serious crimes had been committed, but they by no means warranted the panic that seized the Trudeau government.

To understand that panic, the two kidnappings must be seen within the political context in Quebec where the independence movement was gaining ground. The idea of an independent Quebec germinated quite inauspiciously in 1960, but it quickly took root and by April 1970 the Parti Québécois achieved its first electoral success. In that general election, it won seven seats in the Quebec National Assembly but with twenty-three percent of popular support. Quebec independence had also received international attention, particularly from an eminent political figure of the twentieth century, General Charles de Gaulle, who threw his support behind Quebec in 1967. While the movement was steadily making headway—and perhaps because of that—the rest of Canada, and Quebec federalists, were scrambling to provide answers. Never a decent word could be heard about separatism, and, more often than not, political leaders would rival in their injurious hyperbole. Whenever the federal civil servants spoke out about it, their leitmotiv was that of "sedition" or "subversion" as illustrated in the Mackenzie Commission Report. For political leaders, the movement was described in terms of "deranged minds" or even worse, as in the case of Pierre Elliott Trudeau, "a crime against humanity."[1]

The "October Crisis" resulted from the combined effect of the two kidnappings and the federal government's anger at seeing the independence movement constantly gain momentum.

• • •

War measures were devised for war. Whence the name of the act that was introduced in our political lives in August 1914. War measures were invoked during the First World War 1914-18 and again during the Second World War 1939-45. Curiously, they were not invoked during the Korean War, nor during the years of fear that marked the Cold War and the rampant McCarthyism. Under the War Measures Act, the federal government can use all the powers that it deems useful—and it alone is judge—to achieve its goals. The government is not required to obtain either an opinion or authorization from anybody. In other words, war measures entitled the federal government in the twentieth century to say exactly what Louis XIV said three centuries earlier, "L'État, c'est moi."

The War Measures Act concentrates power in the hands of a tiny group of people, sometimes in one man's hands, as was the case with Mackenzie King in 1940. Civil liberties and judicial rights are suspended, censorship is applied, and suspicion, distrust, and denunciations run rampant. It becomes very easy and common to arrest and detain people incommunicado simply because they have, or are suspected of having, ideas deemed to be dangerous by the government. They have no right to their day in court before a judge or even to communicate with a lawyer. That was how communists and fascists were locked up between 1939 and 1945, and how Jehovah's Witnesses, who had the unfortunate practice of believing in peace, were interned. That

---

1. "A crime against humanity... that would send a shockwave of disbelief around the world," said Trudeau before the United States Congress on February 22, 1977.

was how Italians in Quebec and Ontario were interned during the Second World War. And that was how the federal government settled scores with what it considered to be an ethnically closed community of Japanese on the West Coast: 22,000 Japanese Canadians were sent to camps for the entire war and more, and were never again able to reorganize as a community. (See James Eayrs in Chapter 2.) The War Measures Act was also used to combat the anti-conscription movement in Quebec. The spectacular arrest and four-year internment without trial of Camillien Houde, Mayor of Montreal, then Canada's largest city, was a severe warning to anybody who might be tempted to oppose conscription. The War Measures Act is based on unbridled authority, fear, and the threat of violence.

That act was invoked in the middle of the night on October 16, 1970, at 4 a.m. to be exact. Soldiers had already been deployed in Quebec. It is important to remember that invocation of war measures and recourse to the army are legally two distinct operations. The army can be called in without the war measures being proclaimed, as was the case in Oka in 1990 when the army was mobilized to help put an end to that crisis. The War Measures Act and its regulations declared that the FLQ was illegal and that it was crime to be, or to have been, a member. The prime minister provided three official reasons for invoking the act: the kid-nappings, the request made by the government of Quebec, and "con-fused minds." These reasons are curious and suspicious. As Reg Whitaker points out in Chapter 5, the RCMP was opposed to invoking the War Measures Act as a means to free the two hostages and arrest the kidnappers. Though the Quebec government provided a letter, it is well known that Pierre Elliott Trudeau was never one to automatically give in to Quebec's demands. And finally, since when and in what coun-tries is there no "confusion" as long as democracy and freedom of expression exists? Was Prime Minister Trudeau nostalgic for the old days when Duplessis enjoyed triumphant "unanimity?"

Over and above the massive deployment of troops—7,500 patrolled Montreal alone—what were the impacts of the war measures in the field? Arrests were massive (at least 450 people). People were often arrested "in the middle of the night," sometimes quite violently, as Cruickshank shows in Chapter 6.[2] The lists used to arrest people had

2. "It took away the requirement that police officers act reasonably," wrote euphemistic-ally University of Saskatchewan Jurist and Professor Schmeiser, 1971, 4 Man. L.J. 459.

nothing to do with the kidnappings. More than ten thousand homes were searched, very often "in the middle of the night" as was the case for Parti Québécois organizers in Drummondville according to Jacques Parizeau's biographer. [3] (In Chapter 6, Nick Auf der Maur tells of at least two of his friends whose homes were searched while he was being arrested.) The backdrop to the arrests and searches was the "fear, panic, and hysteria" that gripped Quebec, but also Ottawa, Toronto, and the West, thousands of kilometres away where no FLQ member could be expected to hole up. Jack Granatstein and John Conway describe the atmosphere that reigned in English Canada. Last but by no means least, it must not be forgotten that Pierre Laporte was killed the day after the War Measures Act was invoked, on October 17, at about 6 p.m., and his body was found in an abandoned car six and a half hours later, at 12:30 a.m. on October 18.[4] Those were the short-term impacts of the war measures. The long-term impacts on our hearts and minds, and more specifically on our political system, have not yet been established. Some authors, such as Robert Stanfield, Hugh Segal, and Margaret Atwood, have nonetheless expressed serious concern about them.

• • •

The year 2010 marks the fortieth anniversary of the October Crisis. Political passions appear to have waned and politics in Canada are calmer now. New age groups and new generations are now a majority in the country. Their knowledge of that period and those events is sketchy, if they know anything at all. The time has come to revisit the 1970 war measures. If not now, when?

Our memory of the crisis is largely dominated by a number of facts and images: Pierre Laporte and his death, the FLQ and its dishevelled

---

3. Pierre Duchesne, *Jacques Parizeau, Tome I Le Croisé 1930-1970*, Québec Amérique, Montreal, 2001, pp. 570-571.

4. The kidnapping of Pierre Laporte partly explains the war measures, but his murder does not. If any link is to be made, it must be considered a result of the proclamation of the War Measures Act. People in Quebec, including journalists and political person-alities—Pierre Laporte was both a journalist and a politician—have widely debated whether or not everything must be done to save a human life. Trudeau had no such compunctions even concerning his wife and tiny children. He made that very clear to his wife, Margaret Trudeau, who spoke about it in her memoirs *Beyond Reason,* Margaret Trudeau.

and sinister-looking members, the solitude of James Cross, troops in the streets of Montreal, and Trudeau's "Just watch me." Most of us are familiar with those facts and images since they are the core of the films, photos, and narrative of the crisis. They automatically spring to mind when the "October Crisis" is mentioned and, in fact, inform our memory of the crisis. Moreover, the media and the public at large systematically repeat them. (Readers are invited to ask their friends and colleagues, "What do you know about the October Crisis?" The answer will undoubtedly be an enumeration that begins with the death of Pierre Laporte.)

Our approach is different. The starting point is Trudeau's "Just watch me" and our goal is to understand what such an arrogant and threatening statement really meant. In a nutshell, we hope to get off the streets of Montreal—and Saint-Hubert, where Pierre Laporte was held—and get a "view from the top." New pieces to the puzzle have been found (i.e., memoirs of politicians, release of erstwhile confidential documents, academic studies) and they provide new insight and take us beyond the conventional narrative.

This task is not easy since people have chosen to forget. Robert Stanfield, head of the Conservative Party and Leader of the Opposition in 1970, was chagrined to observe that, "The public enthusiastically approved, and since then never wanted any account." Forgetting can be the easy way to get over what Robert Fulford called "A profoundly shameful moment in our history," what Eric Kierans termed, "That lamentable period of Canadian history," and what Ramsay Cook described as "that doleful October." The upshot is that every time October comes around, we are left sitting passively listening to the story about James Cross and Pierre Laporte and about how the FLQ was pitted against the combined police forces. It has become the *Bonnie and Clyde* story of Canadian politics. Sometimes it's exciting, sometimes sad and even tragic at the end, but it makes no sense at all. To begin the narrative with Pierre Laporte means that it will end with Pierre Laporte. Our memory of events remains locked up, gagged, like he was, in the trunk of a car. As long as our memory remains safely locked up, nobody is bothered, and especially not the powers that be, which in Canada, as elsewhere, count on our collective amnesia to ensure impunity.

The shame—or guilt—about October is palpable, at least in Quebec and particularly among sovereigntists. Perhaps it stems from the very goal of the authorities in 1970, which was to link the FLQ and its crimes to the Parti Québécois. Can it be posited that this shame or guilt was, and remains to this day, the ultimate and unquestionable victory of censorship imposed under the War Measures Act?

We will only comprehend the shame and its mechanisms when we have been freed from it. That is why, as editors of this anthology, we chose to study what was said and written in English Canada, based on the notion that the feelings of shame or guilt had not numbed people in English Canada as much as in Quebec, even though both were equally concerned and involved in the events. All documents but one in this anthology were written or spoken by English Canadians. Lucien Saulnier, Chairman of the Montreal City Council Executive Committee, is the exception, along with Pierre Elliott Trudeau himself. Since the documents or speeches originated in English, we are publishing them in English preceded by well-indicated editors' notes. It is hoped that a French version of this book will appear in the near future.

Another reason prompted us to look towards English Canada for answers. What Quebecers saw coming from English Canada during the 1970 October Crisis, and what they heard and still remember, are the massive means deployed, especially by the military, buoyed up by a tidal wave of blind, angry, and hostile sentiment. A people were on the march to war, and happy to be so—"frisch und froh" was how the enemy described it in 1914—a people immunized against doubt, united, monolithic, applauding and urging their government along.

This potent picture reflects what happened during the first weeks quite accurately. It has dominated, and continues to dominate, Quebecers' collective memory of the October Crisis and has become just one more case for blaming "*les Anglais*," who supposedly marched unanimously against Quebec and Quebecers. That is what is said to have happened during the Patriotes' revolt in 1837 and 1838, and during the referendums of 1980 and 1995.

We know however that things did not happen that way in 1837. We know that Papineau led a rebellion in Lower Canada (Quebec) and Mackenzie led one in Upper Canada (Ontario). Moreover, more people were executed in Upper Canada than in Lower Canada following those revolts. Our hypothesis was that most likely a similar phenomenon occurred in October 1970, and that the monolith was in fact riddled with cracks. We believed that there were people in Parliament, in the media, and among the population at large in English Canada who refused to march to the Trudeau government's drum. Some may not have stood up in October 1970, but they spoke out later to set the record straight. Our hypothesis was well founded. Many English Canadians spoke up, acted, reflected, and above all wrote, with much less unanimity, with nuance, and sometimes in strong opposition to the official truth. By noting, stating, and revealing this difference, even forty years later, we can cast some doubt on and perhaps even overcome the notion that "they" stood united against Quebec. That objectionable notion hampers our ability to establish good neighbourly relations and continues to isolate Quebecers.

• • •

Trudeau's Darkest Hour presents the writings or speeches of twenty-five authors. They include politicians from the Trudeau cabinet, ministers Don Jamieson and Eric Kierans, and from the Opposition, beginning with New Democratic Party leader Tommy Douglas, undoubtedly the hero during that "doleful October," but also Robert Stanfield, leader of the Conservative Party, David Macdonald, Conservative member of Parliament from Prince Edward Island, and Grattan O'Leary, a prominent journalist who had been appointed senator. Hugh Segal, now a senator after being a senior advisor to Brian Mulroney, is another Conservative who in 1970 was a student leader. Hugh Segal provides his thoughts on the crisis after reflecting on it for twenty-five years..

Journalists also made important contributions. Nick Auf der Maur was editor-in-chief of the left-wing review *The Last Post* and host of a CBC television program in 1970. He tells the story of his arrest and detention. Robert Fulford was among the first to denounce the Trudeau government loudly and clearly in the prestigious *Saturday Night* magazine. Several years later he was equally incensed when he reviewed the fictional film *Les ordres* on the imprisonment of citizens in October 1970. James Eayrs was a university professor who spoke out against the war measures in his columns published in two major dailies. (His candour cost him his column in the *Montreal Star.*) Peter C. Newman was the *Toronto Star*'s editor-in-chief in 1970 and he found himself in Trudeau's closest circles during the tense period when the prime minister was imposing the war measures. He recounted that episode in detail in a book published in 2004. In a 1980 feature marking the tenth anniversary of the crisis, John Cruickshank of the *Montreal Gazette* told the story of one of the most famous prisoners who was locked up under the war measures.

Academics have studied the war measures. Historian Ramsay Cook appears twice in this anthology, first as a student in 1955 who wrote a thesis about war measures in time of war, 1939-45, and then in a book of memories in which he provides his impressions of Pierre Elliott Trudeau. Jack Granatstein was a history professor in Toronto in 1970. He experienced a particularly dramatic event during the first days of the crisis and wrote about it many years later. John Conway, a university sociology professor from Saskatchewan, makes the case that the war measures left scars all across Canada. Reg Whitaker, a York University professor who specializes in security questions, published a detailed study of RCMP activities and intelligence before and during the October crisis. In a similar vein, military historian Desmond Morton looked into the organization of Canada's armed forces. His observations reinforce those provided by Canadian Army Officer Dan Loomis who was "on the ground" with the army in 1970. The part of the book on the police and the army is complemented by documents from the Mackenzie Commission on Security and parliamentary testimony by Lucien Saulnier, who was Montreal Mayor Jean Drapeau's right-hand man.

The war measures came to be through an act of Parliament, but an act that is a departure from the normal rule of law. Jurists have studied the question over the years. The Canadian Bar Association wrote some very enlightening material about war measures in time of war in 1944. After 1970, Thomas R. Berger, a lawyer and a constitutionalist, wrote about the war measures crisis while he was still a judge on the British Columbia Supreme Court.

Many citizens shaken up by the crisis spoke up collectively in opposition to the war measures. In one case some fifty personalities of all political stripes and from all regions in the country made their position known in a pamphlet entitled *Strong and Free*. In another case, twenty well-known people in the Toronto region signed a public statement in opposition to the war measures.

Many writers of poetry and fiction refused to remain silent about October 1970. They are represented in the poems published in the wake of the crisis by Margaret Atwood (*Saturday Night*) and Mervyn Procope (*Canadian Forum*).

• • •

Forty years later is the perfect time to refresh our memory, for if we don't do it now, we may never do it. Otherwise one hundred years could go by and October 1970 will have become little more than a distant memory with no real political meaning, as was the case with *The Riot that Never Was* in 1832 or the burning of the Parliament in Montreal in 1849.

Forty years later is the ideal time to answer "present" to all those who, as early as 1970 or in the years that followed, hoped and demanded that the memory of those events remain alive. In 1975 Robert Fulford wrote, "We still need to know a great deal more about what happened to Canada and its collective life in that period. The sad fact is that we forget much too easily." That same year Denis Smith, editor of the *Canadian Forum*, wrote, "We cannot allow ourselves to dismiss the memory and implications of those days (…) the world is still a place of terrorism and Canada possesses no special immunity (…) How well are we prepared to respond again?"[5] By helping us understand what happened in 1970, each author or political personality in this anthology beckons us to refresh our memories. This book hopefully provides a worthy response.

---

5. Denis Smith, "Forgotten Folly," *Canadian Forum*, October 1975.

1

MARKING HISTORY

**"The struggles of Canada's minorities and dissenters (...)
throw into relief the true extent of the Canadian capacity
for tolerance and of our belief in diversity."**

Thomas R. Berger

◆

EDITORS' NOTES

The October Crisis fits into history, draws meaning from that history, but also must stand to be compared with other similar events. When war measures were invoked in 1970, they inevitably reminded people of the war measures in time of war between 1939-45, and particularly how they were used against Japanese Canadians. Ramsay Cook, James Eayrs, and others made that comparison aptly. It is in fact no wonder that people spontaneously remembered the war measures that were applied in the Second World War since only twenty-five years had gone by and many of the players and observers in the 1970 crisis had intimate memories of their previous use. (In comparison, forty years have gone by since October 1970.) As young militant opponents of conscription, for example, Mayor Jean Drapeau of Montreal and Prime Minister Pierre Elliott Trudeau had learned that the War Measures Act was a real threat to political and human rights. Mayor Drapeau's predecessor, Mayor Camillien Houde, who was also a member of the Quebec Legislature at the time, was rounded up in August 1940 and interned for four years because of his opposition to conscription.

Some observers went back even further in our collective memory. Thomas R. Berger is a British Columbia legal expert who has specialized in Constitutional and Aboriginal law. In 1981, he published *Fragile Freedoms, Human Rights and Dissent in Canada*[1] in which he reviewed eight of the darkest moments in Canada's history as regards rights and freedoms. One such moment was the October Crisis, "Democracy and Terror: October 1970," the title of a chapter. Five chapters address episodes of collective rivalry pitting the English against various minorities. In the eighteenth

---

1. Thomas R. Berger, *Fragile Freedoms, Human Rights and Dissent in Canada*, Clarke, Irwin and Company, Toronto/Vancouver, 1981

century, "The Acadians: Expulsion and Return"; in the nineteenth century, "Louis Riel and the New Nation"; at the turn of the twentieth century, "Laurier and the Separate Schools"; in the twentieth century, "The Banished Canadians: Mackenzie King and the Japanese Canadians"; and most recently, "The Nishga Indians and Aboriginal Rights." In addition to these cases of collective rivalry involving what he termed "minorities," Berger provided two cases of ideological dissent, both of which occurred in the twentieth century, "The Communist Party and the Limits of Dissent," and "Jehovah's Witnesses: Church, State and Religious Dissent."

Thomas Berger's matrix for analysing the October Crisis was therefore that of "minorities" and "dissenters." One must ask: did the October Crisis concern a "minority" or "dissenters"? Some contributors to this anthology opt for the former, others for the latter. Perhaps both came into play. Readers can make up their own minds.

Thomas Berger was born in 1931 and was called to the bar in 1957. During the 1960s he went briefly into provincial politics and was elected member of the British Columbia Legislature for the New Democratic Party. He was appointed to the Supreme Court of British Columbia in 1971, where he remained for twelve years. During his years on the Bench, he headed three royal commissions, including the Mackenzie Valley Pipeline Inquiry. Based on the recommendations of that inquiry, Berger became known as a champion of Aboriginal rights. His public dissent on that issue at a time when Trudeau was trying to push the new Constitution through led to his unexpected resignation as a judge.[2]

Thomas Berger's book is by no means only a litany of "darkest" hours since the conflicts described also provided Canada with heroes. Each episode described by Berger gave rise to a hero of the time, from those that took place a century earlier, like Riel and Laurier, to more modern heroes like judges Ivan Rand and Emmett Hall. Only the war measures crisis of 1970 failed to produce a hero in Berger's eyes. Most likely, Thomas Berger wanted his readers to discover the real heroes of 1970 for themselves.

◆

---

2. Here is how he described his resignation in his autobiography: "This notoriety (as a champion of Aboriginal rights) was to lead in 1983 to my departure from the bench. When Canada's new Constitution and Charter of Rights was adopted, I publicly protested the abandonment of those provisions that recognized the rights of the Indians, the Inuit and the Metis. Those same provisions were restored, but I was chastised by Prime Minister Pierre Trudeau and by Bora Laskin, then chief justice of Canada. I left the bench and returned to law practice in Vancouver." Thomas R. Berger, *One man's justice, A Life in the Law*, Vancouver/Toronto, Douglas and McIntyre; Seattle, University of Washington Press. 2002.

In Canada, we have two great societies, one English speaking, one French speaking, joined by history and circumstance. When we look to our past, we can see that the central issue of our history has been the working out of relations between these two societies. No discussion of Canadian institutions can proceed except as a discussion of the evolution of relations between the English and the French on this continent. The dominant theme of the constitutional discussions that led to Confederation in 1867 was the accommodation of these two communities in Canada. This theme, though sometimes it recedes, still overshadows the continuing constitutional debate of our own time.

These two societies, today, have much in common. Both are urban, industrial and bureaucratic. Although their linguistic and cultural differences are still significant, and they are responsible for the creative tension that is the distinctive characteristic of the Canadian political scene, these differences no longer threaten either side. As Pierre Trudeau has remarked, "The die is cast in Canada. Neither of our two language groups can force assimilation on the other."

It was not always so. The conquest of New France by the British in 1759 led to a series of attempts to assimilate the people of Quebec. These attempts were stoutly resisted by Quebecers, and their population of 60,000 has grown to some six million, and their culture flourishes as never before. The history of the French Canadians of Quebec epitomizes the struggle of minorities everywhere.

Today, in every Canadian province, there is a minority that speaks either English or French, and this fundamental duality places the condition of minorities at the very centre of our institutional arrangements. At the same time, the diversity of our huge nation has given rise to many forms of dissent.

This book [*Fragile Freedoms*] is not, therefore, about Laval and Frontenac, Wolfe and Montcalm. It is not about Confederation, the Canadian Pacific Railway, and the North-West Mounted Police; nor is it about Canadian achievements in the First World War and the Second World War. Instead, *Fragile Freedoms* is about the expulsion and return of the Acadians; it is about the destruction of the Metis as a nation and the loss of their homeland on the plains; it is about the school crisis in Manitoba, when French Canadians were denied the right to separate schools, and the school crisis in Ontario, when the French Canadians were denied the right to speak their own language in their own schools;

it is about the internment of the Japanese Canadians during the Second World War and their banishment after the war; it is about measures taken against Communists to curb their freedom of speech and of association; it is about the persecution of the Witnesses of Jehovah in Quebec; it is about the internment in 1970 of hundreds of dissidents in Quebec during the October Crisis; and it is about Native rights and the land claims movement of today.

This is a book, then, about minorities and dissenters, about their struggles, their victories, their defeats. But this book is also about Canada and Canadians, for the victories and defeats of our minorities and dissenters are, in their own way, the history of the successes and failures of our institutions: of our Parliament, our legislatures and our courts; and of our politicians, our judges, and ourselves.

Of course, the struggles of Canada's minorities and dissenters do not by any means represent the whole Canadian experience. But they throw into relief the true extent of the Canadian capacity for tolerance and of our belief in diversity. They sharpen our perception of ourselves. Although many of these struggles began long ago, they still continue, and may have a contemporary denouement.

Some Canadians regard our history as a burden and consider that here are only tiresome tales of events long past. How can we progress, encumbered with this historical baggage? Why should we be reminded of these dark passages in the Canadian journey? Is there no end to our *mea culpas*? Today, we are a prosperous and peaceful nation, we have stable institutions, we admit to full citizenship persons of all races, of any religion, of every language. What is past is past. Our only obligation, as President John F. Kennedy said, is to be just in our own time.

But to be just in our own time often requires an understanding of earlier times. The world was not invented this morning, and we cannot comprehend what measures will supply justice in our own time unless we understand the history of times past.

The Canadian Constitution has always recognized that we are a plural, not a monolithic, nation. This is one of the finest Canadian traditions. Refugees from every continent, immigrants of every race, peoples of all faiths, and persons seeking political asylum have all found their place in Canadian life. It is our good fortune not to be of one common descent, not to speak one language only. We are not cursed with a triumphant ideology; we are not given to mindless patriotism.

For these reasons Canada is a difficult nation to govern; there is never an easy consensus. Yet, our diversity shouldn't terrify us: it should be our strength, not our weakness.

Along every seam in the Canadian mosaic unravelled by conflict, a binding thread of tolerance can be seen. I speak of tolerance not as mere indifference, but in its most positive aspect, as the expression of a profound belief in the virtues of diversity and in the right to dissent.

Many Canadians have championed the ideal of tolerance throughout our history. Who can forget the tortured figure of Louis Riel, who died insisting upon the rights of his people? Or the great Laurier, pleading the cause of the Franco-Ontarians during the First World War? Or Angus MacInnis, who insisted upon the rights of the Japanese Canadians during the Second World War when the whole of British Columbia—in fact, the whole nation—stood against them? Or John Diefenbaker, calling for an end to the persecution of the Jehovah's Witnesses during the Second World War; Pierre Trudeau, defender of civil liberties in Quebec during the 1950s under the Duplessis regime; Ivan Rand, a great judge and legal philosopher, who affirmed the rights of political and religious dissenters during the 1950s; and Emmett Hall, whose humane judgement in the Nishga Indians' case in 1973 opened up the whole question of Native claims in Canada?

I am not urging that we set up a national waxworks. But the Canadian imagination is still peopled almost exclusively by the heroes and heroines of other nations, and our knowledge of who we are has suffered as a result. The crises of times past have thrown into prominence many men and women who have articulated and defended an idea of Canada that has illuminated the Canadian journey. These Canadians—men and women of courage and compassion—were committed to an idea of Canada that we can all share today, an idea that goes deeper than the division of powers, an idea more eloquent than any set of constitutional proposals, an idea that took root long before the present crisis and which will endure beyond it-a faith in fundamental freedoms and in tolerance for all people. This idea of Canada represents the highest aspiration of any nation, and it evokes the best in our Canadian traditions.

2

WAR MEASURES IN TIME OF WAR

"The roots of liberalism have not grown deep in the arid
soil of Canada's heterogeneous community."

Ramsay Cook

◆

EDITORS' NOTES

Ramsay Cook is a well-known historian whose personal memories about
the October crisis can be found in Chapter 8. Yet Cook had taken an interest
in war measures and their effects on our democracy very early in his career.
In fact, he devoted his master's thesis to the question, defending it at
Queen's University in 1955.[1]

In his thesis, Cook criticized the repressive measures used during the
Second World War by Mackenzie King and his two successive justice ministers, Ernest Lapointe and Louis Saint-Laurent. Above all, he deplored how
weakly Canadian public opinion responded to war measures. On this point,
Ramsay Cook heralded other similar positions taken by authors in this
anthology such as David Macdonald, Robert Fulford, Robert Stanfield, and
Hugh Segal. Nonetheless, Ramsay Cook's 1955 explanation in reference to
Canada's political history and ethnic make-up is unique and, to our knowledge, has not been present in the debate on war measures in 1970.

The final words in his thesis written fifteen years before Trudeau proclaimed the war measures are particularly interesting: "Canadians have
always expressed pride in their British heritage. It would be a sorry outcome of this vaunted pride if, in the face of some future crisis, Canada
should lose her British liberties."

◆

1. Ramsay Cook, *Canadian Liberalism in wartime; A Study of the Defence of Canada
Regulations and Some Canadian Attitudes to Civil Liberties in wartime*, M.A. Thesis,
Queen's University, 1955.

By virtue of the power vested in it by the War Measures Act of 1914 the Government clothed itself with authority broad enough to rule by order-in-council, with no obligation to report its activities to parliament. Unlike Britain, where orders-in-council had to be placed before parliament within twenty-eight days of their passage, in Canada there was no guarantee that the House of Commons would be allowed to scrutinize all Government actions. Under the Defence of Canada Regulations, which have been the main concern of this study, the Minister of Justice was provided with adequate power to suppress all criticism of the Government of the day. Though these powers were never pressed to the maximum lengths of their capacity, their very existence, as potential weapons of a dictatorship, is a serious criticism of the Government's liberalism. The fact that public opinion failed to take this challenge to the people's traditional liberties in any forceful fashion is an indication that the existence of liberal precepts in Canada has a tenuous and unsound foundation. People who found that their own civil liberties were not seriously curtailed showed little or no concern for minority groups whose rights were completely denied. Thus a start was made down the path to totalitarianism.

Particularly in the period prior to the revision of the regulations in the summer of 1941 the government pressed these regulations to a point which exceeded the real demands of the situation. Prior to the 1941 revision the checks placed on the government's power to promote "the safety of the state and the efficient prosecution of the war" were exceedingly weak, if not entirely absent. It must be conceded that in time of war, some extraordinary powers must be vested in the executive branch of the government to ensure the internal security of the country, but this concession does not allow that control over these powers be taken completely out of the hands of parliament.

It is here contended, that the drastic curtailment of civil liberties set in motion in September 1939, by the King Government, was made possible by indifference or lack of faith and understanding of liberal institutions on the part of the majority of the Canadian people. The Government took the initiative by accepting and implementing regulations framed by a group of civil servants. This Committee of civil servants, by including a member of the RCMP in its complement, in effect allowed the police to contribute to the framing of laws, whereas, traditionally the task of the police is merely in the enforcement of laws framed by the civil arm of government. The fact that the government and the people accepted this new departure is surely a reflection on our docility and inexperience in the operation of liberal institutions.

In initiating the stringent security regulations, a government, which called itself Liberal, must stand condemned in the eyes of those who are fully committed to the principles of liberal democracy. But to place the entire responsibility at the feet of the government is to see only the outward manifestation of a fundamental vice. The responsibility for the illiberal security regulations belongs to the King administration but the action was accepted by a large majority of the Canadian people, though it cannot be said to have been requested by popular opinion. Protests and criticisms of the measures came from relatively few politicians, newspapers, periodicals and private organizations. The majority of the Canadian people indicated their acceptance, if not approval, through silence. At the same time, no government regarding itself as the custodian of the British liberal tradition, could have been blind to what it was doing, and thus cannot escape criticism. The conclusion to be drawn from this situation is that the roots of liberalism have not grown deep in the arid soil of Canada's heterogeneous community. The question remains as to why Canadians have failed to embrace more faithfully the liberal tradition so handsomely provided for them.

Since Confederation Canadians have drifted a considerable distance from their English liberal heritage. Canadians in general seem less wedded to the doctrines of liberalism than their forefathers from Britain. This is explained, at least in part, by the fact that our tradition is inherited. Canadians, at least since the days of Papineau and Mackenzie, have never had to struggle against great odds to win their freedom from arbitrary government. Our rebellion against an irresponsible executive in 1837 attracted little support and was easily crushed; 1837 does not live in our tradition like 1649 does in Britain's or 1775 in the heritage of the United States. Our "bloodless revolution" of 1849 has been prosaically described to Canadians as the "winning of responsible government." (...)

The challenges to our liberty have not seemed sufficiently serious to produce any heroic response and our memories of any challenge have been dimmed so as to weaken our power to recognize the challenge when it arose in the form of the Defence of Canada Regulations.

In addition to the fact that the liberal tradition has grown weak among those who are direct lineal descendants from its source, there is the fact that our population has been increased by hundreds of thousands of people to whom this tradition is almost wholly foreign. People of all nations have come to live in Canada, and though they have often expressed the desire to live in the "land of freedom and opportunity," few were familiar with the historic struggles out of which our freedom gradually evolved.

The presence of this large group of new Canadians, whose experience is outside the pale of the liberal tradition, had a twofold effect on Canadian liberalism during the war. Firstly, few of this group would have much of a realization that the principles underlying the Defence Regulations were in large part completely contrary to liberal judicial processes and institutions. Therefore, little in the way of protest against these arbitrary security measures could be expected from this group.

In addition, the cosmopolitan nature of the Canadian community seems to have caused the Government serious concern about the loyalty of some alien groups. In an effort to meet the potential threat posed by alien groups, the Government provided not only for the internment of people who came to Canada from enemy countries, but also prescribed methods for the incarceration of such groups as the Japanese Canadians who had lived their entire lives in Canada. The presence of these aliens was given as one of the reasons why the Canadian regulations had to be more stringent than those in Britain where the population was more homogeneous. (…)

Nevertheless the influx of non-British immigrants into Canada provides only a minor explanation for the weakness of our liberal tradition. The fault lies with ourselves, not with foreigners for it must be remembered that many of our British settlers were those with whom the liberal tradition was weak. Those from Northern Ireland and even United Empire Loyalists represent an intolerant tradition which placed "loyalty" far in advance of liberty. From these groups came the illiberalism and intolerance represented in the Loyal Orange Lodge. It is therefore a superficial view which attributes the weakness of our liberal tradition to foreigners. The fact that the most stringent application of the Defence of Canada Regulations took place in Ontario, Canada's most "British" province, is witness to this misapprehension.

Though the liberal tradition has been weakened by a failure or inability to keep it virile under Canadian conditions, it has not become a wholly uninfluential factor in the conduct of our political life. As we have seen, there were groups and individuals organized to protest against undue infringements on civil liberties and these groups acted in the best tradition of liberalism. All the protest groups were small (though labour congress protests represented large groups, it was only a small group of labour men who took a keen interest in the debates on the subject at the annual conventions). And led largely by intellectuals. It is no doubt true, however, that even in the most liberal societies, it is always a minority, the Pyms and the Hampdens, which has to take the action in demanding safeguards for freedom and civil liberty. These groups which came forward to protect against the arbitrary features of the security regulations, and whose members were courageous enough to do so at a time when the state of public opinion made their activities most unpopular, made an important contribution to the preservation of Canadian liberal institutions.

Both Lapointe and St. Laurent, as French Canadians and therefore, conscious of the repression to which a minority may be subjected, should have recognized the futility of placing faith in a government whose law depended on the will of a single man.

On no occasion did a French Canadian member of parliament object to the Defence of Canada Regulations or to any specific regulation on principle. The only objections raised were to the internment of Montreal's Mayor Houde. The case of Houde was surely a graphic example of what might have happened to many more French Canadians, yet no Quebec M.P. showed any realization of the potential danger of the situation. The relative indifference of French Canadian politicians and the fact that both Ministers of Justice were French Canadians and were equally impervious to the criticisms of the regulations based on liberal principles lends weight to the contention that the majority of French Canadians have never been thoroughly divorced from the French legal tradition. The genius of the Common Law has not penetrated deeply into the French Canadian legal tradition. Stated more simply, the French Canadians have never wholly accepted the precepts of British liberalism; their main concern has been with group or minority rights rather than with individual rights against the Crown.

In summing up, it is apparent that the wartime government in Canada was overzealous in its anxiety to guarantee the country's internal security, and with the exception of a few notable and important pockets of resistance, the people of Canada docilely accepted the curtailment of their liberties. (…)

In a period of war crisis an atmosphere is created which makes such abnormal powers very dangerous, for public opinion, verging on hysteria, may force a government to proceed to unforeseen lengths. Therefore it is of supreme importance that the powers of governments be checked both by the traditional judicial processes, and frequent meetings of parliament. In wartime Canada, not only did the security regulations set aside some of the traditional judicial checks, as was the case with Regulation twenty-one but the limitation provided by parliamentary criticism was often absent for periods of unjustifiable length. This is particularly true of the earlier years of the war; the regulations were in force from September 1939 to June 1940 before parliament was given an opportunity to subject them to the hygienic light of free criticism. Thereafter they were discussed annually, while in the intervening period the government was free to enforce new regulations without any necessity of consulting the House of Commons, either before or after the action was taken. Such a situation is difficult to justify on any grounds and is certainly a blatant denial of the principles of parliamentary government.

This partial denial of liberal institutions in Canada during the Second World War tends to invalidate in some measure the thesis that the war was a struggle between freedom and tyranny. Though Canada did not become a wartime dictatorship, the traditional rights and freedoms of some minority groups such as the Jehovah's Witnesses were denied, while other freedoms were seriously curtailed or threatened by the introduction of such concepts as "preventative detention" into Canadian legal processes. The existence of the War Measures Act and the Defence of Canada Regulations provided machinery which could have been easily used as the first solid stepping stone down the path of totalitarianism. (…)

Canadians have always expressed pride in their British heritage. It would be a sorry outcome of this vaunted pride if, in the face of some future crisis, Canada should lose her British liberties.

"Canada's record of resorting to emergency
measures shows them to have
been monuments to folly."

James Eayrs

◆

EDITORS' NOTES
We generally study history to avoid repeating past errors.

That was surely what Professor James Eayrs had in mind—that and his desire to limit foreseen damage—when he devoted his column in *The Toronto Star* in October 1970 to the war measures and specifically to how they were used between 1939 and 1945. He insisted on two points, the treatment of Japanese Canadians and censorship.

a) Eayrs is not the only author in this book to recall what was done to Japanese Canadians during the war. Thomas Berger, Tommy Douglas, and Hugh Segal also made that link. Nor were they alone in underscoring the following similarities. Parliament was obedient—only one member of Parliament, Angus McInnis of the CCF (the forerunner to the New Democratic Party) had the courage in 1942 to denounce measures taken to evacuate the Japanese. Men of the law remained silent—not a single lawyer among the many MPs who were also lawyers dared to oppose Mackenzie King. Public opinion was unbridled and hysterical: "I remember being booed off the platform in Vancouver for opposing that," recalled Tommy Douglas about the events of 1942. Eayrs pointedly drew attention to the very troublesome fact that the heaviest sanction was decided upon *after* and not during the war, namely to deport Japanese Canadians to Japan. This action was particularly serious since the government was in effect erasing the distinction between time of war and time of peace, and thus conditioning opinion in a manner that would later allow the government to resort to the War Measures Act again in peacetime, which it did in 1970.

b) As regards censorship in time of war, Eayrs recalls that it was done on a "voluntary" basis. "The law was there, and it was severe, and editors needed to take heed of it, but they were under no compunction to go near the press censors." He also recalls that job of censorship was given to sea-soned journalists: "A hateful task to mutilate the copy of one's colleague." He concluded that there were "No brutal operations (…) It was all very Canadian."

James Eayrs was a university professor and a specialist in international relations. As of 1960, he devoted time to journalistic writing with columns in both *The Toronto Star* and *The Montreal Star*. The war measures in 1970 became the subject of no less than six columns between October 1970 and October 1971. Five of them appeared together in a collection of his columns published in 1973 under the title "The unnecessary crisis." The article below was the second in the series.

Freedom of expression and of opinion suffered severely in the fall of 1970. James Eayrs' columns on the war measures in *The Montreal Star* were his last, since the Editor-in-chief put an end to their relationship "in cir-cumstances that would baffle a Kafka." The exchange that followed is enlightening about the darkness that prevailed in the fall of 1970. Editor-in-chief Frank B. Walker tried to justify his actions: "In the October crisis [Eayrs] was both strident and malicious in his comments on those charged with greater responsibility and more instant decisions… One of his better efforts over that long, cold, bitter month…still contains in it that high-pitched note which falls somewhere between a snarl and a whine."

To which Eayrs replied: "A whine is an unlovely sound, and I am sorry to have been thought to have emitted it. But there was much to snarl about. As to shrillness I plead guilty—though in circumstances I believe extenu-ating. One must remember the deep diapason in which *vox populi* throbbed its assent as the Canadian government stripped us of our civil rights: over such a threnody, if you weren't shrill you could not be heard."[1]

En 1980, Margaret Atwood made the following remark: "If you think that Canada is really a democratic country where the freedom of expres-sion exists, you must remember the War Measures Act."[2] She was probably thinking about what James Eayrs and others had experienced.

◆

"The government decided to introduce a new bill with as wide powers as were granted before (…) They followed the course of face-lifting (…) But the same tell-tale wrinkles are there, the same wrinkles that

---

1. James Eayrs, *Greenpeace and her Enemies*, Toronto, Anansi 1973.
2. See Chapter 7.4.

spell dictatorship in this country if we do not oppose the granting of these powers to the government."

So John Diefenbaker thundered against replacing the War Measures Act by the Emergency Transitional Powers Act in December, 1945. A quarter of a century has passed, and Dief's speech is as serviceable as ever. Hardly a word need have been changed, hardly a metaphor unmixed, for it to have been used last week to attack the replacement of the War Measures Act by the Public Order Temporary Measures Act [i.e., Turner Bill].

But in the bellies of the Tories the fires have gone out. The old chief is an extinct volcano, his leader has not yet been known to erupt. The NDP has crumpled in the crunch, as socialists always seem to do. Only an isolated Prince Edward Islander, David Macdonald (PC-Egmont), saved Parliament from shame.

Canada's record of resorting to emergency measures shows them to have been monuments to folly.

Using the War Measures Act, the federal government early in 1942 deprived all "members of the Japanese race" whether Canadian citizens or not, of their jobs, their domiciles, their properties, their liberties. A livestock building in Vancouver served as a reception centre for some 22,000 men, women, and children on their way to work camps in the interior.

Not since the expulsion of the Acadians had there been such mass injustice. "The bitterness, the anguish, is complete," wrote T. M. Kitagawa to the custodian of Japanese properties after the government had sold the home from which he and his family had been forcibly evicted. "You who deal in lifeless figures, files and statistics could never measure the depth of hurt and outrage dealt out to those of us who love this land. It is because we are Canadians that we protest the violation of our birth-right." Will those Quebeckers imprisoned without charge or reason these past few weeks emerge with their patriotism so unscathed?

V-J Day brought no restitution to Canadians of Japanese descent. Their pleas before the Supreme Court of Canada and the Judicial Committee of the Privy Council were quashed by jurists more impressed by the division of power than by the loss of human rights. They remained wards of the state, citizens with no recourse to justice. Three years later they were still unable to travel freely in British Columbia or to fish along the Pacific Coast—restrictions, a study of their predicament noted in

1948, which "will undoubtedly disappear with the final expiration of the extension of the war powers of the government." These were not permitted to expire until 1954.

Another war measure was censorship. Here was more of an indignity than an injustice. There were no brutal operations against press rooms, few pre-emptions of the airwaves. It was all very Canadian. "The censorship system was voluntary," the man in charge of it has explained. "The law was there, and it was severe, and editors needed to take heed of it, but they were under no compunction to go near the press censors (…) If we examined material and expressed the view that it violated the law, an editor could still go ahead and print it and take the risk, if he chose."

An odd country. It now seemed free, or nearly so; but appearances were deceptive. A secret order-in-council, passed on Oct. 6, 1945 under the War Measures Act and kept in force under the Emergency Transitional Powers Act, allowed the minister of justice to hold without trial anyone suspected of acting in a manner prejudicial to the public safety.

Scores of Canadians were accordingly detained for alleged spying for the Soviet Union. But Igor Gouzenko, clerk in the Soviet embassy who went to the RCMP, not the order-in-council, deserves credit for apprehending the guilty parties. Half of those imprisoned were later acquitted in the courts. "The arbitrary character of this piece of subsidiary legislation," write R. M. Dawson and Norman Ward in their latest edition of their political science text, *The Government of Canada*, "and the degree to which it abrogated some of the most cherished rights of the citizen afford the best illustration of how extreme was the authority which had been delegated by Parliament to the government." The best, but far from only illustration. Orders-in-council became the order of the day, rule by fiat replaced the rule of law. On Dec. 16, 1947, Parliament debated yet another bill by which the Liberals were to cling to wartime powers. The CCF supported it; only the Conservatives were opposed.

J. M. Macdonnell of Toronto led the Tory attack. "We who have been free, moderately, are asked to put shackles on ourselves. We who have struggled for generations to achieve the position of living under the rule of law are now to live to a very large extent under the arbitrary powers of one man… It may well be asked how people who called themselves Liberals were ever brought to agree to this."

Across the aisle, Prime Minister W. L. Mackenzie King gloomily asked himself the same question, for the cabinet had drafted the bill to C. D. Howe's specifications during King's absence overseas. "A pretty telling reply," King wrote in his diary of Macdonnell's speech. "He is quite right in his criticism of powers being given Howe under the act. They are far too arbitrary and quite contrary to the Liberal method (...) Both he and the government will regret these features of the bill."

Emergency powers are here again. The case against them stays the same. Nothing that needs doing can't be done without them. Much that should not be done is done on account of them. The evil that they do lives after them. The good are oft interned by means of them.

Where then to find a place to stand? Dealing with the dilemma of liberal democracy confronted by the terror of a super-power, retired U.S. diplomat George Kennan offers advice even more helpful to a liberal democracy tempted to resort to repressive legislation to counter the terror of a tiny band: "Let us divest ourselves of this weapon altogether; let us stake our safety on God's grace and our own good consciences and on that measure of common sense and humanity which even our adversaries possess."

> "It is quite reassuring (…) that in time of war
> the central Parliament has full control
> of all property and civil rights."

CANADIAN BAR ASSOCIATION

◆

EDITORS' NOTES

Canada is a federation in which legislative powers are shared by the federal and provincial governments. For the most part, the rules governing the sharing of these powers are established in Sections 91 and 92 of the British North America Act of 1867. Section 91 defines the powers of the federal government, Section 92, those of provincial governments.

By invoking the War Measures Act, the federal government gave itself the right to intervene in provincial areas of jurisdiction as much and as deeply as it deemed necessary and no constituted authority could prevent it. The federal government thus saw its powers, its prestige, and its presence in everyday life increase massively, both in fact and in the collective imagination, while at the same time the provinces experienced a similar but inverse phenomenon. The prime minister could quite bluntly but accurately say to the provinces "L'État, c'est moi!" and you are nothing. From the standpoint of power sharing, the War Measures Act simply shunted the British North America Act aside. The late Frank Scott, professor of constitutional law and a mentor to Pierre Elliott Trudeau, fully understood its scope when he said that the War Measures Act was "Canada's second Constitution." [1]

Some centralizers and ardent supporters of "national unity" surely applauded when they saw power concentrated at the summit of the Canadian pyramid. The Canadian Bar Association and its Committee on Civil Liberties adeptly described that aspect in their 1944 report on the imposition of the War Measures Act. "It is quite reassuring for the preservation of the national life (…) that in time of war the central Parliament

---

1. Robert Bothwell, Ian M. Drummond, and John English, *Canada, 1900-1945*, University of Toronto Press, 1987, p. 381.

has full control of all property and civil rights for the purpose of coping with the emergency."[2]

This tendency of the legal community to accept unquestioningly the War Measures Act appears elsewhere in the report. For example, at one point the Canadian Bar Association publicly expresses its agreement and perhaps even complicity with the government: "We should not assume the risk of embarrassing in the least degree the Government of the country in the paramount task of winning the war."

Some contributors, particularly Thomas Berger, deplored the astounding silence of the legal community when war measures were invoked in 1970. [3] This document from 1944 illustrates that the situation was not very different from that experienced during the Second World War.

◆

CANADIAN BAR ASSOCIATION

Jurisdiction in the matter of Liberties and Property Rights

The civil liberties which we are concerned with cover the wide field of the rights of the subject, and may be, for the purpose of our discussion, considered in relation to three particular objects:

1. Civil and property rights proper, which are more in relation to the civil law as distinct from the criminal law, and cover:
   (a) liberty of religion and language;
   (b) liberty of opinion including freedom of speech, of writing and of the press;
   (e) liberty of enterprise, including freedom of private initiative and industry;
   (d) freedom of work; (e) freedom of association;
   (f) the right to private property;

---

2. *Canadian Bar Association*, "Report of Committee on Civil Liberties," *Canadian Bar Review*, 1944, Vol. XXII.

3. "It is astonishing that in a House of Commons abundantly provided with lawyers, not one of them was prepared to vote against the abrogation of due process on this occasion. But should we be astonished? After all , in 1942, when anti-Japanese sentiment had overwhelmed the country, the only voice raised in Parliament in the defence of the Japanese Canadians was that of Angus MacInnis. The lawyers were silent on that occasion, too." Thomas Berger, *Fragile Freedoms, op. cit.*, pp. 211-212.

2. The protection of the person of the subject, which is more or less in relation to criminal law; and
3. The preservation of the political institutions under which liberties have been acquired and appear to be guaranteed.

As everybody knows, property and civil rights are, in the Constitution, assigned exclusively to the legislative jurisdiction of the provinces, save particular classes of subject matters enumerated in section 91 of the British North America Act. The criminal law pertains exclusively to the Federal power.

The political rights, which are of a varied nature, may, according to circumstances, fall within the Federal or the Provincial jurisdiction.

The War Emergency

It is now settled by the Privy Council that the existence of a state of war shifts from the Provincial to the Federal legislative authority, the power to control Provincial rights and liberties, such as property and civil rights in a Province, inasmuch as it is necessary for the safety of the Dominion as a whole, in case of great emergency, such as the outbreak of a great war.

Though, by section 91 of the B.N.A. Act, the power assigned to the central Parliament "to make laws for the peace, order, and good government of Canada" is, in terms, restricted to "all matters *not* coming within the classes of subjects by this act assigned exclusively to the Legislatures of the Provinces", it is quite reassuring for the preservation of the national life, that the highest judicial authority has so broadly interpreted section 91 to determine that in time of war, the central Parliament has full control of all property and civil rights for the purpose of coping with the emergency.

It is proprietary and civil rights, *in new relations* which they do not present in normal times, that have to be dealt with; and these relations which affect Canada as an entirety, fall within Section 91, because in *their fullness* they extend beyond what Section 92 can really cover.

The kind of power adequate for dealing with them is only to be found in that part of the constitution which establishes power in the State as a whole. (*Fort Francis Pulp Co. v. Manitoba Free Press* (11923) A.C., p. 695.)

It is in virtue of that principle that we now have an abundant Federal legislation, limiting property and civil rights of the citizen, by way of a few acts of Parliament, and thousands of orders-in-council, orders of Boards, rulings of subordinate bodies and civil employees, which have brought a very extensive control, often called bureaucratic, of the activities of the subject throughout Canada.

(...)

Principle and Extent of Control Not Opposed

Whatever opinion anyone might have as to any possible abuse by the Federal authorities, or their delegated boards, of the wide powers so granted to them, and in spite of the civil encroachments this war legislation has developed against the liberty of the subject, your Committee feel that this Association ought not to do anything that might appear to antagonize, or even directly criticize the principle of full control, during the war, of the citizen, his liberty, property and activities, to the extent that the Government deem necessary for the safety of the nation. The Government alone have full information of the necessities of the hour, and however well informed we, of this Association, may be, we should not assume the risk of embarrassing in the least degree the Government of the country in the paramount task of winning the war.

Pierre Elliott Trudeau
on War Measures in Time of War

◆

EDITORS' NOTES
Pierre Trudeau published this letter in defence of Adrien Arcand in 1948 while he was a 29-year-old student at the London School of Economics. Adrien Arcand was the leader of the National Unity Party, the main avowedly fascist and anti-Semitic organization in Canada operating at the time of the Second World War. Arcand was arrested and interned under the War Measures Act imposed by the government of Canada headed by Liberal Prime Minister Mackenzie King. The excerpts below appear for the first time in English along with contextual notes.

◆

"A Letter from London"[1]
"Reflections on a Democracy and its Variant."

In his "Letter from London" Trudeau called Arcand's legal procedure against the Canadian Government to obtain compensation for his internment "a question of absolute fundamental importance" and argued against the idea that "the state of war automatically authorizes a suspension of the democratic rules. On the contrary," he insists:

> If there is a law upon which the citizen has a right to bear judgment, it is that which exposes him to death (...) He has the overriding obligation to keep an even closer watch on his government than at any other time; to criticize without pity those whose increased prestige and work could lead to choose authoritarian solutions. (...) [The citizen] must rise up in

---

1. Pierre Elliott Trudeau, "A letter from London: Reflections on a Democracy and its Variant," in *Notre Temps, Hebdomadaire social et culturel*, Vol. III, No. 18, 14 February 1948, pp. 78-82. Translated by Robin Philpot.

opposition to the idea that a tyrannical law must be condemned in time of peace, but applauded in time of war. (...) The sad truth is that the Liberal government [of Mackenzie King] had its own idea concerning war and was afraid that, after twenty-five years, the people had a different idea. The government did not dare to verify the situation, but rather found it much easier to intern those around whom hostile, or merely critical, opinion might crystallize.

Worse yet, the government proceeded outside the bounds of Common Law and in violation of justice, without due process, adequate defence, known punishment, nor with judgment independent of the executive branch. Thus were violated the fundamental principles of the society of equals; and it went further, since it was even considered illegal for public opinion to side with the victim.

In conclusion, Trudeau condemned the era during which the government of Canada "interned those who did not share its vision of things." He also compared Mackenzie King to the Russian Tsar Nicolas II "who saw the war as an excellent opportunity to suppress opposition and consolidate his power."

Rarely can a person's thoughts be established in more certain terms. Canada was at war. Arcand had unequivocally, publicly, and repeatedly sided with the enemy, Nazi Germany. Yet more than two years after the war had ended and when the evil and barbarian nature of the enemy had become universally known, Trudeau found it "a question of absolute fundamental importance" to consider that the War Measures Act under which Adrien Arcand had been arrested and detained was a "tyrannical law" that "violated the fundamental principles of the society of equals."

Twenty-two years later however, the same Pierre Elliott Trudeau found it absolutely appropriate, in time of peace, to invoke the same War Measures Act to arrest and detain more than 450 people in the same manner, namely without charges, without bail, and without the right legal assistance, and also to conduct more than ten thousand searches without warrants. Barely a handful of these were arrests, detainments and searches were conducted against persons which the Government could reasonably suspect of having collaborated with a declared enemy.

3

THE STAGE IS SET

**"If there is any evidence of an intention to engage
in subversive or seditious activities, or if there
is any suggestion of foreign influence..."**

The Royal Commission on Security

◆

EDITORS' NOTES
The Mackenzie Commission was established late in 1966 to study problems
of "security." Maxwell Weir Mackenzie of Montreal chaired the Commission,
which also included Major James William Coldwell of Ottawa, and Quebec
City lawyer Yves Pratte. It submitted the *Report of the Royal Commission
on Security* to the government in the fall of 1968 and an abridged version
was published in June 1969. The excerpt below "Quebec Separatism and
Security" is taken from that publication.

The Commission observed that in addition to communism, which
remained a threat, "a second and perhaps more difficult internal security
problem" had appeared, namely "separatism." Theoretically, this problem
might not be a real threat on the condition that there were no "subversive
or seditious" elements and that there was no foreign interference.
Unfortunately, the Commission stated, both elements were present and
active. "There is no doubt about communist and Trotskyist interest and
involvement." As regards foreign influence, "It is clear that certain communist countries have shown a marked interest in the formation of the
Communist Party of Quebec," noted the Commissioners. Were they
thinking of Cuba, which Montreal Executive Committee Chairman Lucien
Saulnier would talk about before the House of Commons standing committee in 1969?

The Mackenzie Report made no mention of French influence on the
independence movement, even though France had become a priority
during the Commission's mandate after General de Gaulle visited Quebec
in July 1967. In fact, Prime Minister Lester B. Pearson had convened an
emergency meeting of Security Council on August 14, 1967. Moreover, at
the very time the report was being submitted to the government in
September 1968, Prime Minister Trudeau made a public charge against a

senior French civil servant, Philippe Rossillon, who was close to indépen-dantiste circles, demanding that he leave Canada immediately. In October 1969, in the famous "Fini les folies!" speech, he also denounced the "red-carpet wars and the consular intrigues," quite obviously thinly veiled refer-ences to France.

◆

21. In addition to the requirement for security procedures imposed by the communist threat, Canada is at present faced with a second and perhaps even more difficult internal security problem arising from the activities of some elements of the Quebec separatist movement. Separatism in Quebec, if it commits no illegalities and appears to seek its ends by legal and democratic means, must be regarded as a political movement, to be dealt with in a political rather than a security context. However, if there is any evidence of an intention to engage in subversive or seditious activities, or if there is any suggestion of foreign influence, it seems to us inescapable that the federal government has a clear duty to take such security measures as are necessary to protect the integrity of the federation. At the very least it must take adequate steps to inform itself of any such threats, and to collect full information about the intentions and capabilities of individuals or movements whose object is to destroy the federation by subversive or seditions methods.

22. Although the more moderate elements of the Quebec separatist movement have up till now been conducting a largely political campaign, it appears to us that there is in certain quarters a tendency to resort to activities that could well be regarded as seditious. What is more, there is no doubt about communist and Trotskyist interest and involvement in the movement. Both groups have established "autonomous" Quebec organizations as somewhat transparent attempts to exploit separatist sentiment; members of both have achieved positions of influence in at least some of the separatist groups and agencies, helped by the often bitter factionalism within the movement itself. For these reasons alone it seems to us essential that the Canadian security authorities should pay close attention to the development of these particular elements of the separatist movement.

23. Foreign involvement is more difficult to establish with any certainty. However, it is clear that certain communist countries have shown a marked interest in the formation of the Communist Party of Quebec.

"That should be enough to show that Canada
is involved in self-destruction."

Lucien Saulnier

◆

EDITORS' NOTES
Montreal was at the heart of the modern independence movement, hence
it bore the brunt of repression under the war measures.

Lucien Saulnier was a Montreal city councillor from 1954 to 1972 and
chairman of the Montreal Executive Committee from 1960 to 1970. He was
Mayor Jean Drapeau's right-hand man when the October Crisis broke out.
He had watched the independence movement develop from being just a
sputter until it achieved real electoral strength. That was why he was
interested in the FLQ and the other groups that he dubbed as "revolutionary." While in office, he experienced rowdy times. In fall 1968, the
language crisis flashed up in Saint-Léonard and it flared up again a year
later with daily demonstrations being held in opposition to the Quebec
government's Bill 63 on language of education. In 1968, a now famous
June 24 parade was the scene of violent confrontation with the police,
who arrested more than four hundred people. After confrontation at the
next June 24 parade in 1969, it was decided that no more parades would
be held in Montreal on Quebec's national holiday (the parade was only
formally reinstated twenty-one years later, in 1990). Lucien Saulnier was
at the Montreal City Hall on July 24, 1967, when De Gaulle made his "Vive
le Québec libre" speech, which showed that, in addition to the government
of Canada, other national governments were closely observing Quebec.

The strike by Montreal police and firemen on October 7, 1969 brought
things to a boil. Demonstrations and confrontations were held daily. (One
demonstrator, who turned out to be a policeman in civil clothes, was killed
after being shot by a sniper from a nearby rooftop.) That day Lucien
Saulnier called in the Canadian Army only to realize to his dismay that
the army was very slow to deploy. Together with Mayor Jean Drapeau
and the Montreal police chief, he sounded a warning at a dramatic press
conference on October 11, 1969: "We now know that in Canada, individuals

and groups are working actively to implement a plan which will carry the destruction of freedom." He then added that, "these individuals and groups are inspired and financed, in many cases, by foreign political powers related to an 'International' that does not share our notion of man's fundamental liberties."

That warning struck familiar chords as it raised questions of foreign influence, threats to freedom, and the "self-destruction of Canada." His message was directed first and foremost to Canada and to the government of Canada itself. A perfect and timely venue was found for Lucien Saulnier in Parliament in Ottawa where a House Standing Committee received him. His alter ego, Michel Côté, lawyer for the Montreal police and for the city, accompanied him before the House Committee. Michel Côté was fully apprised of the demonstrations, arrests, and searches conducted over the past few years. The House Standing Committee listened to them religiously on November 27 and 28, 1969.[1]

Messrs Saulnier and Côté filed their report with more than forty evidentiary exhibits, but they added that this was only a "corner of the curtain." The House Committee lawyer, Claude-Armand Sheppard, cross-examined them and helped bring out the strong points of their presentation. Yes, the RCMP was aware of all this since it was working hand in hand with the Montreal police and it was duly informing the federal government. Yes, in order to make sure the message was heard, Mr. Saulnier had personally informed Pierre Trudeau on at least three occasions, including once privately at Trudeau's home. Saulnier and Côté insisted that security in Canada was threatened, not only politically or ideologically, but also militarily since there was foreign interference. The main foreign influence was Cuba, the country that represented the threatening "International" of which they had already spoken and which had inspired so much fear among Canadians during the October 1962 missile crisis.

It will never be known exactly what impact his remarks had on the decision taken in the middle of the night on October 16, 1970. However, we do know that when Trudeau made his televised announcement about the war measures in the evening of October 16, he spoke of "conspirational organizations," "terrorist organizations," and "systematic terrorism," and he used the word "revolution" three times during his short speech to Canadians ("an armed, revolutionary movement," "violence in the name of revolution," "kidnappers, revolutionaries, and assassins").

It will also never be known what impact the dramatic reference to Cuba had on Trudeau and on his decision to resort to war measures. It should be remembered that Trudeau unhesitatingly used the same threat when

---

1. Standing Committee on Broadcasting, Films and Assistance to the Arts; *Minutes of proceedings and evidence*, Thursday, November 27, 1969; Friday, November 28, 1969.

he went to Washington to mobilize support among public and government opinion in the United States after the Parti Québécois came to power
on November 15, 1976. "Quebec's separation would have much graver
implications for the United States than the 1962 Soviet attempt to place
nuclear missiles in Cuba," he declared at a press conference three months
later on February 23, 1977.[2]

Here is what Lucien Saulnier and Michel Côté said before the House of
Commons Standing Committee, November 27 and 28, 1969

◆

Mr. Lucien Saulnier (Chairman, Executive Committee, City of
Montreal): Mr. Chairman, and members of Committee. I would
like the subject to be clearly understood within its context. I will therefore read some passages that are in the document that has just been
distributed to you, and which reports the observations I made, Saturday,
October 11 last.

We now know that in Canada, individuals and groups are working
actively to implement a plan which will carry the destruction of
freedom, of our form of democratic Government and, in this plan, the
people's will, as expressed in the ballot box, is excluded.

These individuals and groups are inspired and financed, in many
cases, by foreign political powers related to an "International' that does
not share our notion of man's fundamental liberties.

In other cases, the same ideas and the same plan of action are supported by the Government of Canada through *The Company of Young
Canadians*.

For many months now, we have made the seizure of a substantial
quantity of documents which justify the preceding statement with the
greatest certainty. It is enough to-day, and it is my duty to do so, to raise
publicly a corner of the curtain.

The partial revelations to which I will limit myself to-day are but a
small example of things I know and of which I have privately informed
the Prime Minister of Canada a few times in the past year.

These facts justify me to request formally and publicly a public Royal
Commission of Inquiry on the clearly subversive activities of the
Company of Young Canadians.

---

2. Reports on Separatism, Vol. I, No.5, Feb. 16 to Feb. 28, 1977.

The same facts justify the Prime Minister of Canada, while this inquiry is going on, to cut short and without delay any supply of public funds to this organization.

The same facts justify the citizens of Canada to ask their Government to prohibit the use of public funds to support activities of the type which follows:

1. To agitate and organize marches in the educational institutions which bring forth the interruption of academic pursuit;
2. To publish and distribute the names, addresses and phone numbers of industrial workers, thereby identifying them as targets;
3. To infiltrate situations which can develop into major conflicts;
4. To promote social and political strife by teaching the methods of defining inaccessible demands with the admitted purpose of shaking the present social system from its roots;
5. To encourage methods of action (and I quote) which rapidly develop into a revolutionary test of strength;
6. To encourage the occupation of industrial plants during strikes in order to create "head-on-collisions";
7. To distribute written information on communist activities in other countries.

Moreover, the Company of Young Canadians has, in its ranks, in Montreal, more than one member previously convicted, in Montreal, for terrorist activities.

We also find on the premises officially occupied by the Company of Young Canadians and paid for by the Canadian tax payers, newspapers and pamphlets showing how to fabricate Molotov cocktails, paint bombs, flasks, and vials devised to disrupt police work in the maintenance of public order.

These documents recommend fighting men, dogs, and horses with pepper, ball-bearings, and slings and even promote the use of potassium cyanide by way of injection, and these recipes are printed and distributed by the thousands.

All this is contained in tracts, writing, documents, communiqués which are reproduced on equipment bought or rented by the Company of Young Canadians with our taxes. Its paid or volunteer organizers who define themselves as "social animators" roam the Montreal region in motorcars owned by the Canadian people and use them to sow dissention, panic and participate in destructive manifestations.

On the premises which they occupy, at the Canadian payers' costs, children have been recently seen coming out with tracts for distribution or pamphlets for distribution and some of them found on the premises, were heralded with the design of murderous weapons.

Firearms have been found recently on the premises occupied by the organizers of a Company of Young Canadians' project.

That should be enough to show that Canada is involved in self-destruction.

The House Committee then cross-examined Saulnier and Côté.

Mr. Claude-Armand Sheppard (Counsel for the Committee):
In your comments, Mr. Saulnier, you also referred to your worries regarding what you called the "defence of the country." Could you explain more specifically what you meant by this comment?

Mr. Saulnier: Personally, I consider the defence of the country takes two forms: defence in the strict meaning of the term, that is national defence, army, air force, navy, and so on, and also any measures which must be taken in order to prevent the internal destruction of the country's institutions. This is what I mean by the responsibility of the federal government as far as the defence of the country is concerned.

Mr. Sheppard: If I understand you correctly, you reached the conclusion that this defence was inadequate.

Mr. Saulnier: As I said, I noticed on October 7 and 8, that when we are faced with emergency situations such as those we had in Montreal, the country is not in a position to defend itself adequately.

Mr. Sheppard: Are you referring here to a physical defence, a military defence or a political defence?

Mr. Saulnier: I am referring here to a military defence.

Mr. Sheppard: Could you give us more details as to the grounds of your statement?

Mr. Saulnier: On October 7, I had to inform the highest federal authorities, and this I said in public in the middle of the afternoon on the same day, of the situation which we were foreseeing for the evening and the night, the night of the 7th to the 8th, a situation which I called revolutionary. I made a request, then, that all available troops be sent to Montreal. We noticed, that it took more than eight hours to have in Montreal, or near Montreal, a handful of soldiers. And at that time, we had a beginning of revolution in the streets of our city.

Mr. Sheppard: Am I to understand, Mr. Saulnier, that you mean that if an insurrectional situation, such as the one which developed in Montreal on October 7, were to come up simultaneously in several cities, Canada would not be in a position to meet it?

Mr. Saulnier: I am not, of course, in possession of all the information that the Department of National Defence might have, to be able to answer such a question. I shall not hesitate to say that if we were elsewhere to find the same conditions as those prevailing in Montreal on October 7 and 8, all the cities in which such activities could take place would for all purposes be open cities.

Mr. Sheppard: You referred, during your statement, this morning, to the co-operation existing between the Montreal Police Department and the RCMP. Could you, sir, or could Mr. Côté, perhaps, if he is in a better position to give us details, tell us what this co-operation consists of, to the extent that you may do so?

Mr. Saulnier: From the information which I received on several occasions from the Montreal Police officials in Montreal, I gathered that the RCMP as well as the Quebec Provincial Police had the same information, and probably at the same time.

Mr. Sheppard: Am I to understand that all the documents which you tabled today were also in the hands of the RCMP, at about the same time as they were in the possession of the Montreal Police Department?

Mr. Saulnier: Yes, and this is a proof of the co-operation I referred to this morning in my comments. I am told that in several cases they work in the same office and that searches are carried out simultaneously by the various police bodies.

Mr. Sheppard: I note that the majority of the documents which you produced were seized fairly recently, that is, in October of this year?

Previously, let us say before the fall of this year, were your services, already in a position to prepare a file indicating questionable or subversive activities on the part of some CYC volunteers or members?

Mr. Saulnier: Of course, we had some scraps of evidence, some suspicions. I must add that several months ago, the Director of the Montreal Police Department drew my attention to the nature of this information concerning these activities, and he emphasized the aspect which involved the federal authorities. I actually communicated with the highest officials of the government of Canada.

Mr. Sheppard: When was that?

Mr. Saulnier: From memory, I would say it happened from nine to twelve months ago. I informed the federal authorities, namely the Prime Minister of Canada. Since I was advised that the information we had was also in the hands of the RCMP, I suggested that the federal authorities obtain them.

Mr. Sheppard: You mentioned certain documents which would indicate that certain of the volunteers had a deep interest in Cuba. I am wondering whether your investigation brought forth other cases not necessarily pointing to volunteers but that would lead us to conclude that this phenomenon is more generalized and involves more people than the two or three persons mentioned.

Mr. Côté: Mr. Chairman, I will answer this question with your permission. In certain cases the funds come from the Company of Young Canadians. The interest towards foreign countries and as far as Cuba is concerned does exist. And not only were the funds of the Company of Young Canadians used to finance those questionable activities, but there are also private funds involved.

We also have documents that I have read myself and that have been read by the Chairman of the Executive Committee and officials of the federal government that also link other people in other Crown Corporations with Cuba.

These documents have not been brought here because they are but an indication. We would not be able to disclose these documents unless an investigation be held as to the truthfulness of their source. But, however, they lead us to believe that other people in government circles are, as liaison officers (…) in relation with the Republic of Cuba. We have those documents but we cannot table them now, because of the risk of soiling the reputation of the persons involved who might not be related to these activities. But a Royal Commission of Inquiry could do this without any danger to these people's reputation. It is not just Cuba, there are also other countries involved.

Mr. Sheppard: What seems obvious here is that the documents you tabled indicate a certain interest from certain volunteers towards Cuba but they do not prove that Cuba was interested in them. Inversely, has the Government of Cuba shown any interest? Do you have any indications of a two-way communication?

Mr. Côté: Certain documents I have already tabled here indicate that there are certain means of communication. I think it is rather obvious from the file.

We also have other documents that we have not brought with us because they are incomplete but that a Royal Commission could complete and these indications would lead us to believe that foreign countries have been interested in illegal activities of organizations that we have not yet named here and that some financial support had been given to those organizations. I know, after having spoken to officials of certain government services, that their government services are aware of this situation.

Mr. Sheppard: I would like to stick with the Company of Young Canadians. Do you have any indications that contacts have been established with other countries besides Cuba by volunteers or by members of the CYC?

Mr. Côté: Yes.

Mr. Sheppard: Could we ask you to tell us what those countries are?

Mr. Côté: I cannot right now, for the reasons I gave you earlier, give you the name of those countries, because this would neither be useful nor necessary. (…)

Mr. Sheppard: Mr. Côté, although I agree with Mr. De Bané because I gave him the same advice when he was Chairman of the Committee, I am wondering whether you could give the names of countries with whom, to the knowledge of Montreal's police officers, volunteers of the Company of Young Canadians would have had contact.

Mr. Côté: In order to answer this question, Mr. Chairman, I wish to make myself very clear to this Committee, which is an extension of the

House and in all due respect to the Member of Parliament who mentioned the topic, when I said one moment ago that I did not find it useful to mention the name of other countries, this was a personal opinion, but I did not refuse to answer.

If I am ordered to answer I will say that I am bound by Canadian law, but that I am also bound by all laws in this country. One of these laws is that of the Bar of the Province of Quebec. I can say, Mr. Chairman, that I have this information from my client and only at my client's request am I able to give this information. (…)

Mr. Valade: Mr. Saulnier, I would just like to make this file complete. I would like to come back to the relationship between the RCMP, the Provincial Police of Quebec, and the Police Department of Montreal. Can you tell us, what is the mechanism within the police department as far as this co-operation is concerned? Are there joint meetings, or parallel meetings to discuss the various police activities?

Mr. Saulnier: There are details, Mr. Chairman, which Mr. Côté will give you with more accuracy than I can.

Mr. Côté (Chief City Attorney of the City of Montreal): Mr. Valade's question can be easily answered. I can say that the police officers of the RCMP and those of the Quebec Provincial Police occupy offices in our premises in conjunction with the officers of the Police Department of Montreal. When these officers are present at the time of the searches, and they usually are, they participate in the searches carried out by the Police Department of Montreal.

Mr. Valade: When you are faced with a situation which necessarily, or indirectly involves a federal responsibility, do you call on the RCMP to attend and participate in these meetings?

Mr. Côté: This is a joint squad. They are always there. Not only do they have their offices there, but they also have their own telephone lines. These telephone lines are not on the Montreal switchboard but it is their own telephone lines.

Mr. Valade: I am not quite familiar with municipal laws, but when you make seizures, do you have to resort to the assistance of the RCMP, or can you do them without their assistance?

Mr. Côté: No, a seizure is done under the authority of Section 429 of the Criminal Code, through a denunciation made by an officer of the peace, who may be a municipal, provincial or federal police officer. He makes his denunciation as an officer of the peace and obtains a warrant from the judge and he is empowered to use his warrant. But since it is a joint squad and since it is advisable that everyone be informed about what is going on, those matters are usually carried out jointly.

Mr. Valade: Now, as regards the seizure of CYC documents, was the RCMP always present during these seizures or was it done in some cases by the municipal police only?

Mr. Côté: Well, of course, I was not present at these seizures, but I often saw policemen from the three forces coming back to the office with seized evidence.

Mr. Valade: As Chief City Attorney of the City of Montreal, do you call specially on the RCMP when there are subversive activities? Do you mean that subversive activities are the sole responsibility of the Montreal Police Department?

Mr. Côté: The Montreal Police Department can act alone in any matter that does not fall exclusively within the competence of the RCMP, as is the case with subversive activities. But since subversive activities are rarely limited geographically to one city, the Montreal Police Department makes it a point of informing the other police corps.

Regarding one of your previous questions in which you wondered if there were joint meetings, I can answer in the affirmative without revealing any secret. At the higher levels of the police authority, there are meetings which can almost be called statutory. The Superintendent of the RCMP, the Assistant Director of the Montreal Police Department, the Assistant Director of the "security" branch of the Montreal Police, his direct assistant, and the inspectors of the Provincial Police used to meet once a month but now I think it is twice a month. This is really at a higher level. If I am not mistaken, these regular meetings are held every two weeks and there is an exchange of information at each level. Mr. Valade: In that case, regarding the subversive activities, the RCMP was completely informed of what the Montreal Police Department was doing in order to avoid or prevent demonstrations or agitation.

Mr. Côté: Mr. Chairman, what is given now is more or less a conclusion rather than a question. If I were asked if I agree with that conclusion, the answer would be yes.

4

PUSHING WAR MEASURES
THROUGH CABINET

"We did not have a compelling case."

Don Jamieson

◆

EDITORS' NOTES

At least three ministers in the Trudeau government during the war measures crisis answered the question, "Was it justified?" They are Eric Kierans,
Mitchell Sharp, and Don Jamieson.[1] Eric Kierans' description of the events
follows this section. A word about Mitchell Sharp is in order, however,
before we consider Don Jamieson's thoughts.

Mitchell Sharp did not speak publicly about the war measures, but
rather in private, during a one-on-one meeting with his British counter-
part, Sir Alec Douglas-Home. They met in London on November 26, 1970.
As Canada's minister of External Affairs, Mitchell Sharp was discussing the
kidnapping of British Trade Commissioner James Cross and the proclamation of war measures. "There was no evidence of an extensive and coordinated FLQ conspiracy," declared Sharp. He added that the FLQ was no
more than "a small band of thugs; there was no big organization; just a
gang of 'young toughs'." This November 26 meeting was held at the very
time the government Sharp represented was pushing the Turner Bill on
war measures through the House of Commons. Yet Mitchell Sharp's
remarks only became public thirty years later when the Foreign Office
released British government documents unsealed after a thirty-year legal
interim. Despite the passage of time, his admission that it was a hoax did
not go unnoticed. *The Montreal Gazette* ran it as a large headline on
January 6, 2001: "'No FLQ conspiracy,' Canada told Britain," with the
unequivocal subtitle: "While Canadians were being told of an 'apprehended insurrection,' Ottawa was reassuring Britain that the War Measures
Act was 'too broad' for a few young toughs."

---

1. According to Jamieson's and Kierans' memoirs, other ministers as well either "had
grave doubts" or were "obviously troubled," namely Joe Greene, Donald Macdonald,
Gérard Pelletier and John Turner.

Don Jamieson was Trudeau's minister of Transport. He was the first of the three ministers to break the silence on the war measures. He did so posthumously, since he died in 1986 and his memoirs appeared only in 1989. However the passage that concerns the war measures appeared in *Saturday Night* in March 1988 under the title "Overkill." Jamieson was absent on government business when the decision was made on October 15, but he was back and present during the cabinet meeting on October 18 when cabinet ministers obtained a hearing with the RCMP in order to better understand why war measures had been imposed. "We were all shaken very badly by his reply—that, if asked the question, he would have to say that, up to that point at least, he had no such evidence." His memoirs also contain observations about how it was of utmost importance for the federal government to receive a letter from Quebec Premier Robert Bourassa, and how a bitter rivalry between Trudeau and Claude Ryan was being played out. Trudeau is seen by Jamieson to be a prime minister who was defending *his* "national unity," not only against separatists, but also against all Quebec federalists who did not share his own unassailable vision of federalism.

Jamieson's remarks did not escape Gazette columnist Don MacPherson who specializes in Quebec politics. "This posthumous disclosure (…) has received a lot of attention in this province. (…) because it represents apparent confirmation of something (many people here) already suspected." MacPherson added, "Many Quebecers remain convinced more than seventeen years later that the Trudeau government applied the War Measures Act not only to deal with the crisis (…) but also as a psychological ploy to halt the rise of the Quebec nationalist movement." He concluded his column on a philosophical note: "To argue that, even if the government had no evidence of an 'apprehended insurrection,' it was justified in proclaiming the War Measures Act is to argue that the ends justify the means. In this case, those means include misleading the public. (…) In a democracy, governments may not always be able to tell the people the whole truth. But whatever they do tell the people is supposed to be nothing but the truth." [2] Following is an excerpt from Don Jamieson's memoirs published posthumously. [3]

◆

2. Don MacPherson, "October 1970: People weren't told truth," *The Montreal Gazette*, March 16, 1988.
3. Don Jamieson, *A World Unto Itself, The Political Memoirs of Don Jamieson*, Vol. 11, Breakwater Books, 1989.

As to what went on in Ottawa during the next few days, the principal advocate of decisive action, apart from the Prime Minister, was Jean Marchand. Jean had gone to Quebec immediately following the kidnapping of Pierre Laporte. He returned to Ottawa greatly agitated by what he had seen and heard. The Bourassa government, in Jean's opinion, lacked the stability and unity to stand up to the kidnappers and to the FLQ in general. He also feared that there had been widespread FLQ infiltration of various important agencies in Quebec, the ramifications of which could be disastrous.

No doubt the statements he made subsequently regarding the infiltrations of the FLQ and the possibility of widespread acts of terror reflected his genuine and honest assessment of the situation. Probably, it will never be known with certainty just how accurate his judgment was. There can be no doubt, however, that among various groups with whom Marchand had contacts in Quebec, there was real concern, even conviction, that the province was on the brink of anarchy.

Jean Drapeau and Lucien Saulnier in Montreal were among the most vociferous advocates of extreme measures. This is not surprising, particularly in the case of Drapeau, a highly emotional man even in normal circumstances. Another strong influence on Marchand, and subsequently on others, was the intervention of Claude Ryan and various other well-known persons in Quebec. They called for negotiation with the kidnappers, and the meeting of their demands. A few days after my return, Marchand told me personally that Ryan had gone to various influential people in Quebec and had advocated the replacement of the Bourassa government with a provisional regime. This provisional group, Marchand said, was to have been led by René Lévesque. (...)

It had been clear for some time that there was no love lost between the Prime Minister and Claude Ryan. I had also noted during those two and a half years that Trudeau was strongly antagonistic to those who did not share his philosophical approach to federalism or his views on what needed to be done in Quebec. It was evident that among such people as Trudeau, Marchand, Pelletier, and Marc Lalonde, there existed a common antagonism toward various other intellectual elements in Quebec who had been critical of Trudeau's policies and the government's efforts to defuse the Quebec situation. Often, in cabinet and in private meetings, Trudeau made no attempt to hide his scorn for those who, in his view, were inclined to take a soft line in Quebec.

I have no doubt that when he referred during the crisis to the "bleeding hearts" in Quebec, Claude Ryan was one of those he had in mind. It is likely that given this background of antagonism, the Prime Minister was exceedingly irked by Ryan's declaration, especially since it was supported by others such as René Lévesque and a number of union leaders. Their actions undoubtedly evoked a strong reaction in Trudeau, and may have been a key reason for his advocacy of the proclamation of the War Measures Act. (...)

With the benefit of hindsight, however, I am satisfied that from the very moment Cross was abducted, Trudeau saw the incident as an issue on which he could stand or fall, and through which he might be able to assert the federal position in a dramatic manner. Laporte's kidnapping added an important dimension to the crisis, and crystallized Trudeau's position. The Prime Minister saw that if he did not move decisively and immediately, his whole posture regarding Quebec and federalism would lose credibility.

Given this assessment, it is interesting to speculate as to whether or not the decision to proclaim the War Measures Act was influenced more by actual events transpiring at the time, or by a general feeling on the part of the Prime Minister and the Quebec ministers that the crunch had come: if they did not stand up and be counted, it would be the end of their vision of federalism.

During the period of my trip to Paris, the key meeting held in my absence was on the Thursday morning prior to the proclamation of the War Measures Act. There was a very heated discussion about the possibility of proclaiming the Act, and the Prime Minister, the Quebec ministers and some others were prepared to take immediate action. In fact, they were willing to introduce most of the extreme measures permitted under the statute. Joe Greene, John Turner and one or two others had grave doubts about the wisdom of proclaiming the Act at all. Primarily on their insistence, the decision was made that the measure would not be activated until a formal request for its proclamation had been made by the Quebec government and by the municipal administration of Montreal. Once this compromise had been agreed upon, the die was cast, and, of course, the rest is history. (...)

My main contribution to the special meeting was an expression of my feeling that the main task that lay ahead of us was to cope with the inevitable claims that the government had acted irresponsibly, or had overreacted, in proclaiming the War Measures Act. In my judgment, the credibility issue would be the main one to surface once the original emotional response to events had subsided. I felt that this was particularly true in the case of the NDP; having gone out on a limb in criticizing the proclamation of the Act, its one defence would be to show that the measure had been unnecessary in the first place. I pointed out also that the news media, having gone along with us almost unanimously, would be asking us to prove our case. I felt strongly that someone should be at work documenting the various developments and supporting them with facts to the maximum extent possible.

The Prime Minister was surprisingly unresponsive to this suggestion. He did not argue against it specifically; on the other hand, he did not act to set up a task force to provide a rationale for the government's actions. Subsequent events made his reason for nonresponse very plain. It was his growing awareness, and perhaps concern, that very little in the way of concrete evidence was going to turn up.

I have the feeling that even as early as that Sunday, there was a suspicion in the Prime Minister's mind, as there was in the minds of many of us, that many of the claims made by spokesmen on the issue had been highly coloured and based on exaggerated rumour. For example, there had been reports that radio-controlled vehicles loaded with dynamite were to be placed strategically in Montreal, and their explosive cargoes set off by remote control. Nothing to confirm this report had been turned up by police. There had been no discovery of large stores of dynamite or weapons in the hands of the FLQ. Nor could evidence be publicly documented that would assert without question the existence of an organized plot.

When the War Measures Act was proclaimed, there was widespread hope within cabinet that the police sweeps authorized by the Act would, within a day or so, provide us with the kind of evidence that would justify the action we had taken. By Sunday, however, nothing significant had turned up; nor had the police captured Laporte's killers or tracked down Cross and his abductors. In other words, conditions on Sunday were not significantly different than they had been before the War Measures Act went into effect. There was no point, therefore, in trying to make a case for the War Measures Act based on hard evidence. This was the main reason for Trudeau's reluctance to initiate any kind of preparatory work on a general defence of our motives.

Like many others in cabinet, I was uneasy over this turn of events. We saw quite clearly what would happen in a day or two when we would be put on the defensive by charges that we had overreacted or, even worse, that we had acted for political reasons or from less than honourable motives. (…)

The meeting with the police was held on Sunday night with most cabinet members in attendance. The Prime Minister, however, was not present. From a police standpoint, it can only be described as a disaster. The officer in charge of intelligence relating to developments in Quebec read excerpts from a paper that was more than a year old. In many respects, it was less precise and complete than many accounts of terrorist and revolutionary activity in Quebec already published in the newspapers and elsewhere. A number of ministers, myself included, questioned the RCMP persistently on their operations. The responses were disquieting, to say the least. The commissioner of the RCMP conceded that the dragnet thrown out following the proclamation of the War Measures Act had produced nothing of any consequence. There had been no discovery of firearms or explosives. Reports of radio-controlled vehicles loaded with explosives had proven to be largely false. Another story about a woman in Hull having been brutally attacked by the FLQ appeared to have been a hoax. (…)

Towards the end of the meeting, the commissioner was asked if what he had been able to uncover both before and after the proclamation of the Act would be enough to support a claim that an insurrection was being planned. We were all shaken very badly by his reply—that, if asked that question, he would have to say that, up to that point at least, he had no such evidence. The implication of such a statement is obvious. If stated publicly in such a bare fashion, it would provide all the ammunition needed by our critics who had argued from the beginning that the invocation of the War Measures Act was unjustified. Seeing our startled reaction, the commissioner went on to say that, of course, he was referring solely to the police failure to uncover the large supplies of explosives, ammunition and firearms that were allegedly in the hands of the FLQ. He added that there was, in addition to the known thefts of dynamite and other explosives, and the known activities and writings of leaders of the FLQ, a general climate of unrest within Quebec. In the judgment of both himself and his officers, the total pattern was sufficient to justify the government's actions. At this point, I began to realize more than I had previously why Trudeau had not moved quickly to accept my suggestion that we try to prepare a rationale or defence of our actions. Clearly, he had been given the same type of background information by the RCMP, and had realized that in concrete terms, we did not have a compelling case to put forward.

"Our common sense went out the window."

Eric Kierans

◆

EDITORS' NOTES
Two cabinet ministers recounted what happened when the Trudeau government decided to impose war measures. Don Jamieson showed how flimsy the case was and Eric Kierans corroborated his observation. "There was no secret knowledge. Everything we were told came from the streets outside." However, Kierans also added that the hysteria in the streets also overwhelmed the cabinet ministers. "We were as swept-up in the hysterical coverage of the FLQ activities as everybody else." He recalled the remarks made by George McIlraith and Jean Marchand as well as those of Marc Lalonde, who was not even a cabinet minister: "things look bad, very bad indeed." Even the remarks made by Justice Minister John Turner fuelled the hysteria: "It is my hope that some day the intelligence upon which the government acted can be made public."

Faced with such apparently drastic circumstances, unsurprisingly the entire Liberal caucus was caught up in the panic. That panic gave rise to some very aggressive behaviour according to one member of Parliament who spoke to reporter Peter Reilly. "I thought I was sitting with a bunch of Mussolini blackshirts. You should have heard some of the opinions being expressed. I kept sinking lower and lower in my chair, and thinking 'these are my fellow Liberals'."[1]

Eric Kierans was born to a working-class family in Montreal in 1914. After studying economics, he became Director of the School of Commerce at McGill University and then Chairman of the Montreal Stock Exchange. The government of Jean Lesage called on him and he was appointed revenue minister in 1963 and then minister of health. As a member of that government during Quebec's Quiet Revolution, he worked closely with René Lévesque. However, when René Lévesque opted for sovereignty-association in 1967, Eric Kierans contributed to Lévesque's departure from the

---

1. Peter Reilly, "The day the Uglies took over politics," *Saturday Night*, December 1970.

Quebec Liberal Party. Pierre Laporte was another of his colleagues in Quebec City.

He then joined federal politics and was elected Liberal Member of Parliament in June 1968. He was a member of Trudeau's cabinet from 1968 until he voluntarily left politics in April 1971, but not because of the war measures. He returned to teaching and died in 2004. In 2001 he published his memoirs entitled *Remembering*, which included his observations about the war measures.

Eric Kierans had many qualities but the most outstanding was his honesty. "Nothing held him back from expressing what he felt was true and just," said former Ontario New Democratic Party Leader Stephen Lewis. "That was a quality which is so rare in Canadian public life that you just got to miss it. Quite apart from the intellect, which was fierce, and the knowledge, which was great, there was that honesty which was searing." His honesty and his unassuming nature permeate the pages on the war measures—"that lamentable period of Canadian history"—as he experienced them in Trudeau's cabinet.

Particularly striking are the harsh words he reserves for fellow minister, Jean Marchand, whom he accuses of being hysterical. "Nonsense," he writes. Kierans is also very critical of Gérard Pelletier whose book in support of the war measures was weak and unconvincing. He also highlights the critical role played by Marc Lalonde throughout that key cabinet meeting on Thursday, October 15. Marc Lalonde was not even a minister, just a political attaché. Eric Kierans solemnly salutes Tommy Douglas's courage in the House of Commons and sadly regrets his own conduct. "If you ask me today why I wasn't up there beside him I can only say, damned if I know."

◆

I did not leave the federal cabinet of Pierre Elliott Trudeau because of the October Crisis. Perhaps I should have, but I didn't. For thirty years I have said very little on that lamentable period of Canadian history, and you will see that I had very little to be proud of throughout the whole affair. It is time to tell that story now, for the first time, from my perspective; then I will go on to talk about the economic issues and issues of governance that sent me out of politics. Readers can decide for themselves whether I waited too long to walk away.

The October Crisis

On Monday, October 5, 1970, at 8:15 a.m., two men gained access to the home of British trade commissioner James Cross, in Montreal's

Westmount, on the pretext that they were delivering a birthday gift. What they carried, however, was not a gift, but revolvers; they handcuffed Cross and bundled him into a waiting taxi, and a bystander heard one of the men say, "We're the FLQ." Soon afterwards, the police received a ransom note containing a list of seven demands, which included publication of a manifesto from the Front de Libération du Québec. The ransom note also demanded the release of twenty-three "political prisoners" whose numbers included convicted terrorists; $500,000 in gold; and the rehiring of *les gars de Lapalme*, as mentioned in the last chapter. They had written out a list of "enemies of the people," on which I ranked in the first ten. They also wanted a plane to fly them to either Cuba or Algeria, with their gold.

The next morning, at a meeting of the cabinet's Committee on Priorities and Planning (I was not a member), Trudeau made it clear that Canada would not give in to these demands, but would keep negotiations open to save the life of James Cross. A message went back to the FLQ (these messages were always left in a telephone booth that the kidnappers would indicate to one of two Montreal radio stations, with the location passed on to the RCMP), rejecting the demands but asking to speak to the kidnappers. They replied that Cross would be killed if their demands were not met by 8:30 a.m. on Wednesday. A series of pre-dawn raids that day resulted in thirty arrests, but no clues as to the whereabouts of the trade commissioner. The 8:30 a.m. deadline was ignored.

The afternoon of Wednesday, October 7, the kidnappers sent along a handwritten note from Cross to prove that he was still alive. That evening, External Affairs Minister Mitchell Sharp, at a news conference, asked that a mediator be named by the FLQ to deal with the federal authorities. The man named was Robert Lemieux, a Montreal lawyer.

On Thursday, October 8, at 10p.m., Radio-Canada met one of the key demands, broadcasting the FLQ manifesto, in French. It was also printed in major newspapers the next day, and turned out to be a nearly illiterate hodgepodge of demands, complaints, and threats.

On Saturday, October 10, Pierre Laporte, a friend and ally from the Lesage government, now labour minister in Robert Bourassa's government, was seized at the point of a machine gun from outside his home on the South Shore, near Montreal. This crime came shortly after Jérôme Choquette, Bourassa's justice minister, had refused to release the prisoners demanded by the FLQ and offered instead to trade a safe conduct to Cuba for the release of Cross. The abduction was immediately described by the media as "an instant response" to Choquette's statement, but it could not have been. The abductors were driving around Laporte's home while the justice minister was speaking. This was the work of an entirely different group of FLQ supporters, who had decided that the seizure of Cross was a mistake; what was needed was a French Canadian hostage. However, the coincidental timing made it appear as if the terrorists were a highly organized, incredibly swift-moving organization.

That night, Premier Robert Bourassa moved into a guarded suite on the twentieth floor of the Queen Elizabeth Hotel in downtown Montreal. This was later made to read that he spent the crisis "cowering in his bunker," although how you got a bunker on the twentieth floor of a hotel was never explained. I knew Bourassa, and I don't believe for a minute that he cowered anywhere. If he went into safekeeping, it was because the police officials responsible for his security told him to do so—how could he have refused?

On Sunday, October 11, while senior officials from Ottawa and Quebec held a series of meetings to plot strategy, Robert Lemieux was arrested, charged with "obstructing justice," and thrown into jail. That night, Premier Bourassa made a speech which seemed to indicate that he was willing to negotiate with the kidnappers; then Lemieux was released from jail and asked to act as their spokesperson.

This was the Thanksgiving weekend; it led to a pause of two days while the police scrambled around, senior bureaucrats met, and not much happened.

On Wednesday, October 14, Bourassa called René Lévesque, who, with Claude Ryan, was pressing the Quebec government to at least consider releasing the prisoners. At this time, René was the leader of the Parti Québécois, formed in October 1968 out of his Mouvement Souveraineté Association and the Ralliement national. He was also the voice of reason.

Ever blunt, René asked the premier, "What the hell's going on? Are you negotiating or aren't you?" Bourassa replied that they were, that he was being kept "fully informed" by the prime minister, and that Trudeau was willing to confirm safe conduct out of the country in return for the release of Cross.

"Jesus Christ!" René exploded. "That's what Choquette said last week!" Bourassa told him that he had a serious split in his cabinet about what action to take, and, he added, "I have the police on my back."

The next day, Thursday, the federal cabinet gathered for its regular cabinet meeting, and it was one of the strangest sessions I ever attended. Trudeau, as usual, was calm, fully in control. Very, very impressive. However, he had very little information to give us. John Diefenbaker, the leader of the Official Opposition, and, before this, ever the defender of civil rights, had asked pointedly in the House whether the government was willing to impose the War Measures Act, a draconian piece of legislation that had been used, and abused, during the Winnipeg Strike and against Japanese Canadians during the Second World War.

Now, it became clear, it was to be imposed again. But the case for imposition was, even within the cabinet room, fuzzy, ill defined, and supported by almost no concrete evidence.

Around the long, oval table in room 205S, the cabinet ministers are gathered, hunched over a pile of documents provided by the Privy Council Office; but we aren't looking at those. We are, instead, looking down the room towards a telephone booth where Marc Lalonde, not a member of the cabinet, but the prime minister's principal secretary, is talking on the telephone to Jérôme Choquette, and every time he comes back from the booth, it is to tell us that "things look very bad, very bad indeed."

When the ministers ask questions, they are answered by Lalonde, not the prime minister, and what he tells us is that Quebec is ready to explode. If swift and stern action is not taken at once, the best information from the best experts is that there will be riots, political assassinations, chaos. There is no question that Lalonde was the dominating figure that morning.

The FLQ had been in existence for six years at this point—this is not something I knew at the time, but it is useful, I think, to consider the background against which we were making our decision. During those years, there had been 200 bombings in Quebec, either by the FLQ or other criminal groups, and a number of holdups to gain money to further terrorist aims. These bombings and holdups had resulted in six deaths, none of which had been a planned assassination.

In contrast, in the fifteen months ending April 30, 1970, there had been 4,300 bombings in the United States, resulting in forty-three deaths and 384 injuries. New York City at this time had a bombing on an average of once every other day.

In our immediate crisis, we had had, so far, two kidnappings. No one in New York was proposing the elimination of all safeguards against unlawful arrest, but that was exactly what we were doing.

The Call For "All-Out War"

Of course, we were as swept up in the hysterical coverage of the FLQ activities as everybody else. Ontario's Premier John Robarts was calling for "all-out war" on the terrorists; newspaper editorials were screaming for drastic action; and police officials were warning us that there was a connection between the FLQ and the militant Black Panther movement in the United States. Later, this turned out to mean that there had been one report in which an informant had two years earlier said there was such a connection.

During our cabinet meeting of October 15, in the two hours before lunch, cabinet members talked around and around the subject, but came to no firm conclusion. I did not speak.

When we broke for lunch, I went back to my office on the ground floor, where Richard Gwyn and Allan Gotlieb were waiting for me. They were both reluctant to see the imposition of war measures, but both insisted that if that was how cabinet was going to go—which it clearly was—it was my duty not to break ranks.

I was heading back up the stairs to the cabinet room when Jean Marchand caught up to me. He said, "How are you going to go on this thing? The prime minister is worried; he thinks you have some doubts. You didn't say anything this morning."

I said, "I don't know. I won't know until I speak this afternoon."

When we got back to the meeting, I was the first on the list, and I said, "I intend to support the imposition of the War Measures Act."

As soon as I said it, looking directly across the table at Trudeau, he raised one hand, in a sort of gesture of triumph, and brought it down over his face. My immediate reaction was, I have just made a terrible mistake. His obvious relief meant that this was not a done deal, there was still some hesitancy about it. I think now that if I had said what I ought to have said, namely that there was no convincing evidence of an "apprehended insurrection," which was the legal rationale for imposing the act, Gérard Pelletier, who was a staunch civil libertarian, and obviously troubled about this, would have bolted as well. There were others, like Donald Macdonald and Don Jamieson, who also must have had their doubts. I am speculating here.

I don't think Trudeau could have pushed it through. What did it, I now think, was the combination of general hysteria outside, and his aura of control inside. At the time, I thought he was fully in command, but in retrospect, he seemed to be almost an observer, rather than a moving force. However, he seemed so damn certain that the course of action being pressed on him by Lalonde was right, that our common sense went out the window, and we gave him backing for what turned out to be a massive injustice—not merely the military occupation of Canadian cities, but the arrest and detention, without charge, of more than 400 Canadian citizens (or, to be exact, French Canadian citizens), who were held without bail. They were beyond the reach of habeas corpus, a right wrenched out of King John at Runnymede, in 1215.

The hysteria was both inflamed and endorsed by such statements as those from John Turner, the minister of justice, that if Canadians generally "knew what we knew," they would understand the need for drastic action. He said, "It is my hope that some day the intelligence upon which the government acted can be made public, because until that day comes, the people of Canada will not be able fully to appraise the course of action which has been taken by the government."

There was no secret knowledge that explained the imposition of war measures. Everything we were told in cabinet came from the streets outside. Turner also argued that "under the present law, the prosecution of this type of violent, criminal conspiracy is rendered difficult, if not impossible, under the present provisions of the Criminal Code."

Pierre Laporte was found murdered on October 17, two days after the imposition of the War Measures Act. James Cross was found and freed on December 3 as a result of normal police surveillance, and his kidnappers flown out to Cuba. Laporte's kidnappers were arrested on December 28, again through the use of ordinary police measures.

Jean Marchand claimed that "these people have infiltrated every strategic place in the province of Quebec, every place where important decisions were taken... this is an organization which has thousands of guns, rifles, machine-guns, bombs, more than enough [dynamite] to blow up the core of downtown Montreal." Nonsense. None of the sudden, secret police raids turned up the guns, rifles, machine guns, bombs, or dynamite, although they did sweep up Pauline Julien, who sang separatist songs.

Gérard Pelletier wrote a whole book, *La Crise d'octobre*, which endeavoured, painfully, to explain why we had suspended the civil liberties of the nation because of two kidnappings. In it, he placed the number of FLQ terrorists at between forty and fifty, backed by 200 to 300 active sympathizers and 2,000 to 3,000 passive supporters, who supported separatism, but not violence. He did not explain how this number of people was going to shred civil order in the province.

When the War Measures Act was proclaimed on October 16, 1970, two reasons were given. The first was that there was an apprehended insurrection, the evidence for which Canadians were to take on faith. The second was that Quebec had asked for the imposition of the act, which was undoubtedly true, but might have been more frankly explained by announcing that the Quebec provincial police and the RCMP were agreed on the suspension of civil liberties, and everybody else went along.

We lost our nerve, and our common sense. George McIlraith got up in the House and solemnly told the nation, "A woman across the river from Ottawa had been kidnapped and the initials FLQ carved on her belly." You would think that might have sent reporters across the Ottawa River to check, but no, they just printed it. My daughter, Cathy, who was working as a school nurse, couldn't go to work because of the crisis; the Montreal school board for which she worked listed her under their "Quarantine Section."

Terry and I were assigned armed soldiers to protect us, as were most cabinet ministers, and there was a great deal of nonsense about this sort of thing. Robert Stanbury, the minister responsible for the newly created Information Canada propaganda machine, was outraged because he wasn't assigned soldiers; they had become a status symbol. He was duly assigned a couple of youngsters with guns to stand on his front lawn. They cross-questioned kids invited to a Halloween party at the Stanbury residence in the Glebe area of Ottawa. ("You say you're a witch, not a separatist? Prove it!")

In a bizarre twist, it became a criminal offence not merely to be a member of the FLQ, but to have ever belonged to that organization, a bit of retroactive legislation that could never have withstood a challenge under the Canadian Charter of Rights and Freedoms—happily, there was no such thing at the time.

It was Tommy Douglas of the NDP who stood in the House, day after day, and hammered the government for suspending civil liberties, and if you ask me today why I wasn't up there beside him I can only say, damned if I know. He showed political courage of the highest order.

DEPLOYMENT OF WAR MEASURES

5.1 Military Deployment

"The government and the military, in 1969, were preparing for a showdown in Quebec."

Dan G. Loomis

◆

EDITORS' NOTES

It is very surprising that with all that has been said and written about the October Crisis and the war measures very little work has directly addressed the military question. In 1970 and since, images of soldiers patrolling the streets of Montreal have often appeared in books and in other media—the cover of this book is an example. Military historians like Desmond Morton have alluded to the military (See Chapter 8, In Hindsight), but in general, parliamentarians and commentators have remained virtually silent. It is a sign of embarrassment that different authors have expressed in different ways. Ramsay Cook complained, "the sight of armed soldiers on the streets of Montreal left me depressed"; while Hugh Segal remarked, "I remain a great supporter of the National Defence Department, but not for its use against our own people. When citizens see armoured vehicles patrolling on a campus in the centre of Ottawa, they know that something is going terribly wrong."

Daniel Gordon Loomis was an officer in the Canadian Army originally from Montreal. He experienced the war measures—"the FLQ emergency," as he called it—as Commander of the Western Quebec region. He closely monitored the two operations: Operation Ginger, launched on October 12 in the Ottawa area, and Operation Essay, which began on October 15 in the Montreal area. He published a book on the subject in 1984, *Not much Glory, Quelling the FLQ*. His description of events shows that the operation had been well prepared and that it relied on well-trained soldiers, some of whom, including Loomis himself, had acquired relevant experience in Cyprus where, as in Canada, two communities confronted each other: "In all, 12,500 troops were deployed as peace officers with over 7,500 going to the Montreal area to reinforce the 10,000 policemen. The army was more prepared for this war than either in 1914 or 1939." He continued: "Almost overnight the highways and back roads of Quebec were filled with military activity; helicopters were flying overhead and the streets were full of armed soldiers in combat kit guarding the residences and offices of potential FLQ targets and vital points, searching for the FLQ kidnappers and performing any number of other tasks associated with the deployment of thousands of troops."

This type of operation could not have been deployed without long and meticulous preparations. Loomis dates those preparations to the Pearson years, and more specifically 1963, immediately following the first wave of FLQ bombs. Preparations were the responsibility of General Jean-Victor Allard, with whom Loomis had collaborated at one point. Loomis identifies a particularly important moment during that process. Four years before the "FLQ emergency," on June 21, 1966, General Allard explained his new philosophy to a delegation of MPs from Ottawa at the Saint-Hubert Command Headquarters. This new philosophy stemmed from the notion "that the major threat to peace and public order in Canada was no longer a foreign power (but) indigenous revolutionary forces bent on destroying the country from within." His exposé went virtually unnoticed in the media even though it was "one of the most far-reaching statements ever given respecting the role of the Canadian forces," and "one of the very few direct public statements describing the preparations for possible insurrection in Quebec."

Loomis devoted an entire chapter of his book to the role played by General Allard, who "was turning the Canadian military into a low-intensity force, ready on extremely short notice to turn its attention to Quebec." To get an idea of General Allard's overall philosophy, one only has to refer to his own statement: "If a man pulls a knife, you do not respond by pulling a slightly longer knife and fighting it out. No, you line up a squad of soldiers with rifles pointed at his heart and tell him to put his knife away or be shot." In the following excerpt, Dan Loomis presents his perception of General Allard's preparations.[1]

◆

Determined as he was to fight the FLQ, Pierre Trudeau needed the support of senior military officials and officers with a strategic concept of policy objectives. Trudeau needed the support of the military; and one man, General Jean Victor Allard, CC, CBE, DSO, ED, CD, was the person he could count on.

---

1. Dan G. Loomis, *Not much Glory, Quelling the FLQ*, Deneau, 1984.

He is, perhaps, Canada's greatest soldier—even greater than Currie, McNaughton and Crerar if one counts the prevention of a war as important as waging war. After winning a DSO and two bars during the Second World War, he spent three years in Moscow—the years of the Gouzenko affair. He was in the Soviet Union as the cold war emerged. By 1953 he was commanding the Canadian Brigade in Korea and within ten years, after becoming the only serving Canadian forces officer to command a British division, he was appointed to the newly-created and key post of chief of operational readiness in the recently integrated Canadian forces headquarters. This was the year in which the FLQ commenced Phase Two of their operations—the mobilization of the people. General Allard's experience as a soldier and diplomat complemented Pearson. Allard was steeped in the writings and experience of the French army both in Indo-China and Algeria. Moreover, his recent command of a British division in Germany had exposed him to dozens of officers who had served in Malaya, Borneo, and elsewhere on counter-insurgency operations. Finally, as a native of Trois-Rivières, Quebec, he was acutely aware of the turmoil and trauma of the "Quiet Revolution" which was transforming the fabric of Quebec society.

He grasped the gravity of the situation as few in the military did, and he prepared for the forthcoming struggle by various means: reorganizing the command structure, redeploying available forces, re-equipping the operational units, and training the field forces. At all costs, what has come to be called a "normative plan" had to be devised to prepare the army and tactical air forces for deterring protracted revolutionary war waged by the FLQ and, if deterrence failed, to fight on as long as was necessary to win.

Allard's thesis of deterrence was direct. He put it this way: "If a man pulls a knife, you do not respond by pulling a slightly longer knife and fighting it out. No, you line up a squad of soldiers with rifles pointed at his heart and tell him to put his knife away or be shot." This was sound advice in terms of the principles of war: selection and maintenance of aim, surprise, economy of effort, and concentration of force. But it could only work once, since surprise was essential for success. In 1970 it worked, saving countless lives in a bloodless victory and more than justifying the award of the nation's highest honour, the Companion of the Order of Canada, by a grateful government. (…)

In a bold move, General Allard located the new command's head-quarters at St. Hubert, on the outskirts of Montreal. In effect, an airhead was established in the projected theatre of operations—a major advantage for deploying air-transportable forces into areas where their landing would be unopposed. It was also close to various police head-quarters in Montreal where liaison would be established, and to Quebec City where, as Regional Commander Eastern Region, General Allard established a full time liaison cell with the Quebec provincial government. (…)

Although many considered Canada's relations with NATO strained, in reality the government and the military, in 1969, were preparing for a showdown in Quebec.

General Allard had been planning his defence for years. As early as 1966, he began publicly briefing politicians on our self-defence preparations. On Thursday, June 21, 1966, just before relinquishing his appointment as Commander Mobile Command to become Chief of Defence Staff, Allard made a crucial presentation to the members of the House of Commons Standing Committee on National Defence. It was a presentation of the concept of operations for the new army and tactical air force—a concept that would have both immediate and long-term consequences for all three services. (…)

Allard began the briefing with a routine review of Mobile Command headquarters and various housekeeping activities. Quickly, however, he turned to the topic foremost in his mind. It would be clear to many by the end of the briefing that, for the general, the major threat to peace and public order in Canada was no longer a foreign power. The threat was, and would be for the foreseeable future, indigenous revolutionary forces bent on destroying the country from within. Forces organized for NATO, Allard stated, are not suited to peacekeeping or peace restoration. (…)

The general described the way these reorganized forces might be used to deter the escalation of agitation and unrest, four years before the October crisis.

In any future peacekeeping or peace restoration operation, we must ensure the most judicious application of our forces is made. Indeed, the opponent normally has the capability of intensifying or scaling up activities with very little effort at the lower end of the scale. Just as nuclear weapons deter all-out nuclear war on the upper end of the scale,

so too, at the lower end of the scale, will the application of the prepon-
derance of force deter the escalation from riots and strike activities into
serious acts of violence and terrorism. The deployment of strong, highly
organized, multi-purpose forces to an area of trouble does not mean
that force will be used; it merely means that a deterrence to more serious
types of conflict will have been achieved.

Within three weeks of this briefing General Allard was promoted
and moved to Ottawa where he took over as chief of the defence staff
on July 15, 1966. Mobile Command was well and truly launched, and
General Allard could get on with preparing the Canadian forces for the
coming showdown with the FLQ.

5.2 Police Deployment

"The RCMP never asked for the War Measures Act, were not consulted as to its usefulness, and would have opposed it if they had been asked their opinion."

Reg Whitaker

◆

EDITORS' NOTES

When a decision as drastic as imposing war measures is taken, it is generally assumed that if the authorities had to call in the army and impose a state of war it was because the enemy was very powerful and that the regular police forces were unable to deal with it.

Reg Whitaker is a political scientist who has studied security questions for many years.[1] He decided to delve into that specific aspect of the 1970 war measures and, under the Access to Information Act, managed to examine many documents that were hitherto secret. He published the results in a long article entitled "Apprehended Insurrection? RCMP Intelligence and the October Crisis," in *Queen's Quarterly* in 1993.

Was the RCMP unprepared, he asked? The first acts of violence by the FLQ were committed in spring 1963 and ended in June 1963. Whitaker observed that the first signs of RCMP involvement appeared on July 22, 1963. Then in 1964, together with the Sûreté du Québec and the Montreal City Police, the RCMP established the Combined Anti-Terrorist Squad. Later that same year they obtained permission to monitor not only the FLQ but also political parties (particularly the Rassemblement pour l'indépendance nationale or RIN) and other "separatist" organizations. They could monitor or infiltrate them using "informers." This work quickly produced results. "One successful RCMP penetration may have begun as early as 1966," he

---

1. Reginald Whitaker was born in Ottawa in 1943. He received his BA and MA in Political Science from Carleton University and his PhD in Political Economy from the University of Toronto. He taught political science at Carleton, York, and Victoria. In 2001 he was named Distinguished Research Professor Emeritus at York University and Adjunct at the University of Victoria. Security and Intelligence are amongst his fields of interest. With historian Greg Kealey, he compiled, edited and published eight volumes of RCMP security bulletins covering the entire inter-war period and the Second World War. He has been professionally active in inquiries into the Maher Arar affair, the Canadian Air Transport Security and the Air India bombing.

notes in referring to the "Taxi Driver," as he was dubbed, "one of the most productive 'human sources'." RCMP infiltration went even further. It is widely known that Claude Morin, who was deputy minister for Inter-governmental Affairs and a close advisor to premiers Jean-Jacques Bertrand and Robert Bourassa (before becoming lead Parti Québécois strategist) "began his career as a paid Mountie informant in 1969."

This police apparatus could certainly not prevent the October 1970 kidnappings. However the following question must be asked: "Did the Security Service provide adequate advance intelligence warning that kidnappings were planned by the FLQ and that people like Cross and Laporte were potential targets?" Whitaker leaves no room for ambiguity on this point: "Here the answer is an unequivocal yes," and he adds that, "in October, the RCMP had the names of most, if not all, of the actual kid-nappers." He then asks the question, "Why was no watch placed on the homes of foreign diplomats in Montreal?"

After years in the field, with some three hundred officers working out of its Montreal detachment, and with informers working from within, the RCMP had clearly understood that it was faced with "a handful of determined youths [who] could wreak destruction and instill fear in the populace," but that there was nothing that resembled a "mass revolutionary base" or an "apprehended insurrection." That is why, according to Whitaker, "the RCMP never asked for the War Measures Act, were not consulted as to its useful-ness, and would have opposed it if they had been asked their opinion."

◆

In the aftermath of the October Crisis, federal ministers from Quebec, including Prime Minister Pierre Trudeau, let it be known that they considered the intelligence on Quebec separatism gathered by the main federal body monitoring internal security—the RCMP Security Service—to have been inadequate, if not worse (Pelletier 157-9; Gwyn 122; Granatstein and Stafford 208). In effect, blame for the Crisis was directed at an intelligence failure. (…)

Blaming the RCMP for inadequate intelligence has not been unani-mous. A minority view has considered that the government should have accepted greater responsibility, and pointed fewer fingers at officials. But accounts critical of the RCMP constitute the received wisdom on the subject. Today, through the use of the Access to Information Act, it is possible to examine some material from the Security Service files and thereby gain greater insight into the quality of the intelligence that the Security Service had gathered. And as is often the case when new documentary evidence becomes available, the received wisdom turns out to require revision.

The 1960s

Demonstrations and graffiti first announced the appearance of the Quebec "national liberation struggle" in 1962. By 1963, acts of politically-motivated violence (bombs, armed robberies) were widespread, claiming two victims (one dead, one severely injured). For the first time in the twentieth century, an organized clandestine group was violently challenging the state in the name of revolutionary goals (see Laurendeau; Fournier). Given the nature of the FLQ'S goals, the federal government, in the form of its security intelligence service, would obviously be called upon for threat assessments. The Security Service was an integral part of the RCMP, which as a federal police force was also concerned with questions of public order and criminal acts such as terrorism. Thus the investigative interest of the RCMP was from the start related both to its security intelligence and law enforcement functions. Constitutionally, it could play only a secondary role to the Quebec provincial police (SQ) and the Montreal city police (MCP) in the latter field, while in the former had primary responsibility. (...)

During its early stages of development, the separatist movement was "not a target for penetration by this Force." Thus, despite early indications of violent potential, the development of the FLQ was "not anticipated." The FLQ bombings were viewed as criminal offenses, and thus prime responsibility fell to the SQ and the MCP: "The RCMP was relegated to a role of assistance when it was requested by the other police forces." If arrested FLQers could have been interviewed by the Security Service right after arrest, "much useful information concerning the FLQ as a subversive organization might have been uncovered." To facilitate coordination of criminal and intelligence information, the Inter-Directorate Liaison Section (IDLS) was set up in early 1964. At this point it became apparent that the separatist movement as a whole had to be assessed, "including the seemingly more moderate sections." There was "considerable effort on the part of the IDLS to locate suitably motivated potential sources for further development"; coverage "has improved and should continue to do so."

The first RCMP threat assessment of the FLQ and other terrorist groups was filed on 22 July 1963, following a wave of arrests. A covering letter to the solicitor general indicated the highly tentative nature of the analysis, which in typical Cold War terms laid heavy stress on possible communist linkages with the FLQ. In 1964 the RCMP co-operated with the SQ and the MCP in the formation of the Combined Anti-Terrorist Squad (CATS), which soon netted further arrests and dealt a heavy blow to the FLQ. By this stage, the federal police were clearly on the ground and running.

In September 1964, a security brief on "Separatism and subversion in Quebec" was prepared by the Security Service and showed a relatively sophisticated grasp of the various currents and factions swirling around the separatist movement. It was an "extremely complex" situation, involving a maze of clandestine and legal organizations that would often splinter or reform, sometimes genuinely but sometimes in order to confuse the police. Another brief in the same month analyzed, in some depth, seven "open" and five covert organizations. Names of individuals in these briefs are censored under the Access Act, so it is difficult to gain an appreciation of the extent of the Security Service's knowledge. (...)

At this stage, the "seemingly legitimate separatist" movement was dominated by the Rassemblement pour l'indépendance nationale (RIN).

At this time the Security Service remained preoccupied with left-wing "socialist" tendencies of the RIN, and the possible connections this might mean with communists. Every use of the term "national liberation struggle" seemed to set off the force's Cold War alarm bells, since this was a phrase widely used by communist or pro-communist Third World revolutionary movements. They admitted there was "not much evidence that separatist leaders have 'openly' co-operated with the Communist party." Separatists, they granted, had no intention of relinquishing control of their organizations to communists, and for their part, the communists did not want to risk the adverse publicity that would come from association with terrorism. Yet the Security Service could not give up the idea that communist influence might be felt in "more subtle ways" that might not even be understood by a substantial segment of the movement In this report there are even nine heavily-censored pages on Trotskyist involvement. An updated version of an earlier brief was subjected to a lengthy critique by Donald Cobb of the Montreal division of the Security Service who insisted that it had failed to fully appreciate the dangers of communist influence over the movement. The paper was expanded and rewritten to reflect Cobb's concerns.

The 1964 briefs had an important policy result. The final version was presented to the Security Panel—the coordinating body that administered government security and made recommendations to cabinet on policy—on 23 September 1964. The RCMP was concerned about a security clearance for a civil servant posted abroad who was an open member of the RIN. The problem was that the government had given no directives to the RCMP indicating that membership in a group like the RIN could constitute a security risk. Yet the RCMP was concerned that there were links between the RIN as an open, apparently democratic, separatist movement, and the terrorist groups like the FLQ. The panel concluded that when conducting security clearances, the RCMP should note in their reports an individual's membership in organizations like the RIN together with such detailed information concerning length of attendance, degrees of involvement, and other pertinent information as was available in order that Departments, on whom final decision for the clearance rested, could consider the necessity of further investigation as they would do in cases of information concerning membership in the Communist Party, Front Organizations or character weaknesses.

Although it was not formalized in a cabinet directive, this decision was crucial for RCMP surveillance of Quebec political life. The Security Panel had given the green light to the Security Service to compile dossiers on separatists legitimately, and it had explicitly agreed that these could include individuals belonging to open and legal groups such as the RIN, as well as to clandestine terrorist organizations, as least so long as the former were suspected of clandestine ties. This also provided opportunities for the Security Service to recruit sources from within separatist groups: the threat of losing a security clearance, and thus a livelihood, could be a powerful inducement to co-operation.

Indeed there is reason to believe that in the mid-1960s the Security Service became much more active in infiltration of the FLQ. Under the Access Act any reference to the identity, or indeed even the existence, of human sources of intelligence is rigorously excluded. However, the quality of intelligence seems to pick up quite distinctly around this

time, as does the level of political analysis. Lists of sources of information, although heavily blacked out in the declassified versions, seem to
indicate that while many open sources were consulted, at least as many
may have been secret. A very well informed writer on the FLQ mentions
one successful RCMP penetration that may have begun as early as 1966.
He speaks of "one of the most productive 'human sources'" recruited
by Donald Cobb in 1968—a source he dubs the "Taxi Driver." This
source enabled the Mounties to draw up organization charts of separatist networks, and to give detailed information on personalities (psychological profiles, meeting places, favourite haunts, etc). Later the "Taxi
Driver" was of considerable assistance during the October Crisis
(Fournier 106).

One limitation under the Access to Information Act is that personal
files are exempted until twenty years following an individual's death.
For events in the 1960s and 1970s, mainly involving activists in their
twenties and thirties, this is a serious barrier. However, one leading
FLQ militant, François Mario Bachand, who was caught up in the first
waves of arrests in the early 1960s and continued as an activist until he
fled Canada in 1969, was subsequently assassinated in Paris in 1971
(under circumstances never satisfactorily explained). Bachand's Security
Service file is now declassified. Through it, one can gain some appreciation of the quantity and quality of intelligence on separatists that was
available to the RCMP. The paper file comprised ten volumes and was
about 2,400 pages in length. A printout of the computer file on Bachand
runs to about ninety additional pages of information coded into such
categories as name, street name, description, property and residences,
itineraries of movements, purpose of movements, outcome of events
he had been associated with, correspondence received, employers,
Unemployment Insurance records, groups involved with, his role in
them, demonstrations attended, etc. "Miscellaneous" includes such
personal matters as "frequently uses propanity [sic], talks about sex in
a smutty manner, not mature and discreet," "has complexes of insecurity
and non confidence in himself," "habitual liar," "only hobby is reading."
Such information could only come from well-placed human sources
familiar with the subject.

The quality of the intelligence is perhaps most apparent in the parts
of the Bachand file relating to his leading role in the *McGill Français*
movement, dedicated to making the venerable anglophone institution

of McGill University into a French language university. Dossiers were sent by the Security Service to the Solicitor General, the Security Panel, and other senior government officials indicating that a mass demonstration at the gates of McGill was to be the cover for a commando raid on the computer centre (this raid was prevented). The Security Service was acting on information gathered on the secret plans of the leadership cadre, among whom Bachand was prominent. They were able to provide highly detailed plans (which rooms to move through to reach the target, how the operation was to be financed— ironically through federal government funds via the Company of Young Canadians). At one large meeting, one Mountie and four Montreal police officers secretly filming the proceedings were detected and forced to leave. But the Bachand file indicates that they had excellent information concerning even small secret strategy meetings; these could only come from a human source.

A threat assessment on "Quebec separatism" at the end of 1969 examined twenty-two organizations from the traditional and very conservative St Jean-Baptiste Society to the radical proletarian Taxi Liberation Movement. By this stage, the Security Service had dismissed the communist bogy as irrelevant, indicating definitively that they had "no evidence" of any communist role. The RIN was now defunct, but there was a much more formidable legitimate arm of the independence movement in the newly-formed Parti Québécois. The Mounties were less than alarmed about this development, at least from the standpoint of revolutionary threats: the PQ, the report indicated, "has scrupulously adhered to an ethically and constitutionally correct approach to the Quebec question"; despite the presence of certain individuals of "dubious political background" there was no evidence of "hostile intelligence activity." The Mounties were interested only in the terrorist and subversive elements: even though the PQ "poses a distinct threat to the integrity of the Federation, it will not be dealt with in any detail." Ironically, the very confidence that enabled the PQ to be set aside stemmed from a source the Security Service had recruited near the very top of the party's hierarchy—the now notorious case of Claude Morin, who began his career as a paid Mountie informant in 1969.

In light of the impending crisis of the following year, which was to call forth the War Measures Act to counter an "apprehended insurrection," the Security Service was coolly realistic about the scope of the terrorist wing, which illustrated, in their words, "dramatically how a handful of determined youths could wreak destruction and instill fear in the populace to a degree highly disproportionate to their numbers." What they did not detect was any indication of a mass revolutionary base.

Another interesting aspect of the 1969 assessment relates to the question of foreign involvement in the separatist movement. Exemptions under the Access Act tend to be particularly frequent where there is any information about foreign governments. One brief on "Foreign involvement in the Quebec separatist movement," which is undated but appears to be from the mid-1960s, contains at least sixty-five pages in the original, but has only about seven left after the liberal application of black ink by censors. It does seem that initially the Security Service was particularly attentive to evidence of communist bloc involvement (not surprising given their Cold War mentality). Cuba was cited as having links to terrorist activity, as was Algeria, then the Mecca for "national liberation movements" everywhere. But communist and other leftist states apparently showed little substantive interest in the Quebec situation. By the end of the 1960s, foreign interest was seen as stemming mainly from France "which has been interfering in Canadian affairs since 1963" (and had done so quite publicly with de Gaulle's infamous "*Vive le Québec libre!*" speech in 1967). Ottawa had already expelled French national Philippe Rossillon, virtually dubbing him an agent of the French secret service. But they never could find the smoking gun of French involvement in the separatist movement (Granatstein and Stafford 200-10). One problem was Canada's lack of an "offensive" intelligence service that might have gathered information on French intentions. The Security Service did try to enlist the help of American and British intelligence, but were politely rebuffed. The search for French interference did, however, offer other grounds for maintaining surveillance, not only of the terrorist organizations but of more legitimate groups like the PQ. The PQ might be a legal party but if the French were seeking to use it for hostile purposes, a watching brief would have to be maintained by the RCMP.

The RCMP and the October Crisis

The charge that the RCMP had failed to provide adequate intelligence to the government is especially focused on the events of October 1970.

If we consider the October Crisis simply at face value as a political hostage crisis, the question of whether the RCMP provided the government with adequate advance warning based on Security Service intelligence can be answered—in the affirmative. It is true that they were not able to prevent the kidnapping of Messrs Cross and Laporte, nor the latter's murder. To suggest that the RCMP had "failed" if they could not prevent the two hostage takings is to set impossible standards for any security intelligence service in similar circumstances (similar reasoning would, for instance, label the British security forces in Northern Ireland as abject failures). A more appropriate question would be: "Did the Security Service provide adequate advance intelligence warning that kidnappings were planned by the FLQ and that people like Cross and Laporte were potential targets?" Here the answer is an unequivocal yes.

A few months after the conclusion of the crisis, the director general of the Security Service, John Starnes, was in the process of reading Gérard Pelletier's *La crise d'Octobre* and came upon a remark by the author suggesting that the police were totally unprepared for the kidnappings of October 1970. Starnes was incensed at this implication of incompetence and asked his staff for documentation on this question. The result was a dossier of evidence to the contrary and a letter from Starnes to Solicitor General Jean-Pierre Goyer, on 14 January 1972, setting the record straight. This dossier makes very interesting reading.

In the first part of 1970 the police foiled two kidnapping attempts, first against an Israeli consul and then against the US consul in Montreal. One of these plots was uncovered by accident in the course of an unrelated investigation, the other by good police work. The Security Service went to some lengths to be sure that senior government officials were aware of the implications of these failed plots. Assistant Commissioner J.E.M. Barette made the point very clearly on 14 April. The combined police forces (RCMP, MCP, SQ) were preparing a contingency plan to cope with any potential kidnappings. Citing the current fashion for political kidnappings among urban guerillas in Latin America, as well as the evidence from Quebec, the Security Service, extrapolated basic target groups. Most likely were foreign diplomats and Quebec political and governmental leaders. Ten days later the director passed on this information to the solicitor general, George McIlraith. Six months later the FLQ kidnapped a British diplomat and a Quebec cabinet minister.

Did the RCMP know who was likely to undertake kidnappings? A document dated 21 May is heavily censored, but *may* be a list of individuals, including photographs, suspected of being possible kidnappers. We know that in October the RCMP had the names of most, if not all, of the actual kidnappers, based on cumulative police evidence and their human sources (the "Taxi Driver," possibly others), but lacked the knowledge of their exact whereabouts. Paul Rose, of the Chénier cell holding Laporte, had been under police surveillance, but this observation was broken through Rose's evasive actions. The RCMP, employing good police work, were able to track down and free Cross, and the kidnappers and killers of Laporte were subsequently apprehended and convicted. The capacity of clandestine terrorist cells to hide hostages in a large metropolitan area, it should be noted, has been demonstrated time and again in various parts of the world, from Beirut to Rome.

The contingency plan set in motion in the spring of 1970 involved a twenty-four-hour hotline to the Department of External Affairs and the FBI liaison, as well as control of movement across borders. Despite warnings, no watch was placed on the homes of foreign diplomats in Montreal, with the result that the kidnappers of Cross met no resistance. If this constituted negligence, it was not the fault of the RCMP but of the government of Canada for failing to take its Security Service's warnings seriously and to offer appropriate protection to threatened foreign diplomats. The kidnapping of Laporte presented an even more egregious spectacle of negligence. With the FLQ already holding Cross, another group of terrorists—who had heard about the diplomat's abduction on their car radio while holidaying in Texas—rushed back to Montreal, drove to the home address of the minister of Labour, found him tossing a football on his front lawn with a nephew, and hauled him into their car. It was a tragic turn of events, but it was not the responsibility of the RCMP to guard Quebec officials.

On December 10, with the crisis over, the Strategic Operations Centre (SOC) set up to coordinate Ottawa's response, took a considered look back (Duchaine v.2). On police and armed forces operations, they concluded that although "certain deficiencies and possibilities for improvement" had been pointed out by agencies themselves, "in general *this was the side of government operations which was best prepared and acquitted itself with great credit*" (emphasis added). Listing the various warnings provided by the RCMP, SOC concluded that "sufficient (although not complete) information was available to forewarn the government of the possibility/probability of an 'October Crisis'" and to "warrant some preventive—or at least preparatory—steps being taken prior to such a crisis breaking out." Why this did not happen was a complex question to which a number of answers could be given. Among these was the "lack of any mechanism for proper *political* evaluation of information put forward by the RCMP, and of any political input to this information" and the lack of political mechanisms to react to this information. This suggests the classic problem of the lack of effective coordination between intelligence agencies and the consumers of the intelligence product, governments. Add to this the "instinctive belief it can't happen here," and we have a recipe for governmental inaction in the face of warnings.

After the PQ came to office in 1976, a special investigation was launched into the events of October 1970 under the direction of Jean-François Duchaine, who reported in 1980. Despite the refusal of the federal government and the RCMP to co-operate with the inquiry, Duchaine was clear that of the three police forces involved, the RCMP was the most knowledgeable and the most professional. It began with numbers: the Security Service had some 300 officers from the Montreal detachment alone, while the combined anti-terrorist forces of the SQ and the MCP amounted to no more than forty-five (this latter number was later augmented). Moreover, the Quebec forces conceded that the Security Service was the best equipped to deal with the situation, while the SQ and MCP had found themselves in a panic, faced with a crisis for which they were largely unprepared. Of the three police forces, the RCMP alone possessed a security service "*d'une certaine ampleur*" (Duchaine 255).

The superiority of the RCMP was nowhere more apparent than in the preparation of lists of detainees to be picked up under the War Measures Act. An initial list was drawn up by Michel Côté, legal counsel to the city of Montreal, in consultation with the MCP, and was used as the basis of the request by Mayor Jean Drapeau for the War Measures Act, but there were not enough names to justify the emergency powers; more names were subsequently added in consultation with the RCMP. The SQ was also expected to contribute to the list, but did not have extensive enough dossiers to do the job; the RCMP Security Service was called in to help. There followed a somewhat bizarre scene:

SQ-RCMP "collaboration" was illusory; the SQ officers were ushered into a room where they were presented with names drawn from files held in another room by the Security Service, files to which the SQ was denied direct access. According to Duchaine, the SQ had no direct knowledge of the information used in the preparation of the lists.

Duchaîne did sharply criticize a certain destructive competition that developed between the RCMP and the two Quebec police forces in the course of the investigations, citing the "strange" attitude of the RCMP toward sharing information with the SQ. Some of this may be attributed to the inevitable, if deplorable, turf wars that always crop up between different police organizations working on the same terrain. There was, however, another dimension to the RCMP's reluctance to share information with the SQ: the Mounties had evidence that the SQ had been infiltrated by one or more FLQ sympathizers (McDonald V.3 203-5).

Another intriguing aspect of the list of detainees is the question of political input. The RCMP arranged a consultation on their list of 158 detainees with two of Trudeau's closest Quebec lieutenants, Jean Marchand and Gérard Pelletier. This was a "gesture of courtesy," but the Mounties were also ready to take advantage of these men's intimate knowledge of Quebec politics and personalities. Both Pelletier and Marchand later leaked to selected journalists an account of this meeting that suggests they were shocked by many of the names and insisted on reducing the list. One account has Marchand crossing out a "ridiculous" name and Pelletier a "few" (Fournier 238). A more expansive version has an "incredulous" and "horrified" Pelletier crossing off "name after name" (Gwyn 118). It is true that the Quebec police, especially outside Montreal, were excessive in round-ups under the special powers, and that the number of arrests did go far beyond the numbers specified in the lists prepared by the Mounties and the MCP. But the retroactive accounts of Marchand and Pelletier are flatly denied by the sworn testimony of senior RCMP officials before the McDonald Commission. Commissioner Higgitt recalled there was "no change." Inspector Joseph Ferraris was explicit: Pelletier had questioned two names but withdrew his objections when they were explained. These differing accounts are mutually exclusive, although sworn testimony before a royal commission does seem more credible than non-attributed leaks to journalists. At stake is the credibility of Security Service intelligence. But as we shall see in a moment, it was not the RCMP that wanted a dragnet under emergency powers, but the government. The list of detainees was as much, or more, to legitimate the decision to invoke the War Measures Act as it was to assist in the police work of tracking down the kidnappers.

The War Measures Act

Two particular versions of October 1970 cast the Security Service in an invidious light. One, citing alleged incompetence, argues that the War Measures Act provided the police with special powers because they could not do the job under normal rules (Mann and Lee 183). The other, stressing a more conspiratorial view of the "secret police," suggests that they seized the opportunity offered by the crisis and the emergency powers to strike a blow against the entire independence movement, especially the PQ (Vallières). Neither version has any basis in fact. The reality is that the RCMP never asked for the War Measures Act, were not consulted as to its usefulness, and would have opposed it if they had been asked their opinion.

Two days before the invocation of the War Measures Act, a meeting of the Cabinet Committee on Security and Intelligence heard RCMP Commissioner William Higgitt suggest that the best course was to continue investigations "as at present." He added that a "broad sweep and preventive detention of suspects" would be counterproductive, leading to "massive problems." He could therefore not recommend the use of special powers at this point in time."

In camera testimony before the McDonald Commission by senior Security Service officials makes clear that the force was "out of the loop" in the decision to invoke the emergency powers. Joseph Ferraris, a veteran of the Security Service (mostly in Quebec) and a member of "G Opts"—the special operations unit—had a key role to play at the time of the crisis. Ferraris later told the McDonald Commissioners that the RCMP and the Security Service in particular thought that the War Measures Act was dangerous in the sense that it "gave too much power." This power was especially misused by local police in Quebec, over whom the RCMP could exercise no control. Worse, he maintained that it probably "delayed our finding Mr. Cross by about two or three weeks, or maybe a month" because it diverted trained manpower from police work to administering the War Measures Act and picking up and questioning people not directly connected to the kidnappings. Ferraris sardonically summed up his impression of the Act: "You don't need an atomic bomb for a riot on St. Catherine Street."

Commissioner William Higgitt was, if anything, even more blunt. He made it clear that he had never been asked for his opinion on the efficacy of invoking the act, but only on the mechanics of implementing it. While he granted that it conferred certain advantages on the police, he added that there were many disadvantages, not least of which were the excessive powers granted the Quebec police and the misuse of these powers that could go on unchecked (many more people were arrested than the RCMP thought reasonable). The commission pressed for documentation of the "apprehended insurrection"; Higgitt said there was none. Indeed, he went further to insist that he would "have stopped somewhat short of using the word *rebellion*" or an "open rebellion"—"I had, I guess, greater faith in the people concerned than that." The commission was puzzled: "it does strike one as passing strange that in what was one of the great crises in this country's history, there was no apparent file opened concerning the apprehension of insurrection." Higgitt was unfazed: "apprehended insurrection" were "words foreign, quite foreign to us as far as I'm concerned."

Here we come to the crux of the issue that lay between the government and its Security Service. In invoking the powers of the War Measures Act, the cabinet was answering formal requests from Quebec and Montreal, but in fact these requests were prompted by Ottawa. If they did not stem from the requirements of the federal police, whence did they come? Even today it is not possible precisely to locate the rationale, but we can say with confidence that the decision came from the prime minister and his inner circle of Quebec ministers and advisers. (...)

In retrospect, from the vantage point of some 20 years later, the outlines of a different interpretation of the events of October can be discerned. All the documentation is not yet available, by any means. But an alternative explanation might go like this: two terrorist cells initiated a political hostage crisis. The RCMP saw the crisis as requiring good, patient, careful police work to solve. The Quebec ministers in Ottawa deliberately chose to escalate the political magnitude of the crisis to justify emergency powers as a means of intimidating nationalists and separatists, with whom the federalist Quebecers were locked in a bitter conflict for the allegiance of Quebec. The October Crisis was in this sense one episode in a kind of Quebec civil war in which non-Quebecers were mainly spectators. The RCMP Security Service was a somewhat reluctant participant and then a scapegoat when the government later found itself in difficulties justifying its actions.[2]

2. Reg Whitaker carefully provided sources, which included: Jean-François Duchaîne, *Rapport sur les événements d'octobre* (2 vols.), Gouvernement du Québec, ministère de la Justice:1980; Louis Fournier, *FLQ: the Anatomy of an Underground Movement,* Toronto, 1984; Richard Gwyn, *The Northern Magus: Pierre Trudeau and Canadians,* Toronto, 1980; J. L. Granatstein and David Stafford, *Spy Wars: Espionage and Canada from Gouzenko to Glasnost,* Toronto, 1990; Don Jamieson, *A World Unto Itself: the Political Memoirs of Don Jamieson,* St John's 1991; Marc Laurendeau, *Les Québécois violents: la violence politique 1962-1972* (revised edition), Montréal, 1990; Edward Mann and John Allan Lee, *The RCMP vs. the People,* Don Mills 1979; McDonald Commission of Inquiry Concerning Certain Activities of the Royal Canadian Mounted Police,*Second and Third Reports,* Ottawa:1981; Gérard Pelletier, *La crise d'Octobre,* Montréal, 1971; Vallières, Pierre, *The Assassination of Pierre Laporte,* Toronto, 1979.

5.3 Political and Media Deployment

"A meticulously concocted lie."
Peter C. Newman

◆

EDITORS' NOTES

In October 1970, Peter C. Newman was editor-in-chief of *The Toronto Star*, Canada's most widely distributed daily paper. He had a solid reputation as a reporter and was intimately familiar with the workings of the federal government and, in this case, had close personal ties with Prime Minister Pierre Elliott Trudeau and Mr. Trudeau's chief of staff, Marc Lalonde. Peter Newman lived through the October crisis with his then-wife Christina McCall, who was also an astute observer of Canadian politics. Neither could be accused of having any sympathy for the FLQ. For all of these reasons, Mr. Newman's description of how things happened and how the highest echelons used and abused their power with the war measures in 1970 is of utmost significance. This story appeared in a chapter entitled "The Gunslinger" in Peter C. Newman's *Here Be Dragons, Telling Tales of People, Power and Passion*.[1] He and his wife were first-hand witnesses to the scenes he so ably describes.

He first describes the strange atmosphere at a cocktail party held by Trade minister Jean-Luc Pépin on October 22, six days after the war measures were invoked. A drunken soldier who was protecting the minister's guests made racist remarks about "crazy frogs" and then scared everybody by casually waving his loaded automatic rifle about and pointing it in every direction. Everybody was then plunged into a surreal world when the forlorn Montreal police chief admitted that their investigations had led them nowhere.

It defies imagination! Six days after the war measures were invoked based largely on Jean Marchand's claim that the FLQ had some 3000 well-trained terrorists armed to the teeth, all of the interrogations, searches, arrests, and the movements of soldiers and fire power of the combined federal, provincial, and municipal police forces and the army had failed to turn up any weapons or armed conspirators, and those responsible had no idea where to look next. Moreover, despite the arrest and detention

---

1. Peter C. Newman, *Here Be Dragons, Telling Tales of People, Power and Passion*, McClelland & Stewart 2004.

incommunicado of hundreds of people supposedly linked to the FLQ, no new clues had turned up. Either those thousands of terrorists were even smarter and better organized than Jean Marchand had claimed—a haunting thought for Pépin's guests that evening—or those dangerous hordes existed in Marchand's imagination only —an even more haunting thought.

One thing was clear nonetheless. The reason given for invoking the war measures, namely that the FLQ's activities represented an "appre-hended insurrection" that threatened peace and good government, was failing to convince anybody. How could an insurrection, "apprehended" or otherwise, remain so elusive when all those means had been brought to bear? Trudeau had to find some other reason.

That was when the "meticulously concocted lie" spawned in the minds of Marc Lalonde, Pierre Elliott Trudeau, and Montreal Mayor Jean Drapeau. It was to be "conspiracy" of eminent Quebecers that included René Levesque, Leader of the Parti Québécois, Jacques Parizeau, President of the Parti Québécois Executive, Marcel Pépin, President of the CSN (Confédération des syndicats nationaux), and Claude Ryan, Publisher of *Le Devoir*. The story would be that they were forming a "provisional parallel government" that would replace Robert Bourassa's duly elected govern-ment by a "revolutionary regime." Newman carefully runs through how he was manipulated and became the conduit by which "news" of the conspiracy was planted in the highest levels of Canadian media. Marc Lalonde, who was "hawk-like in appearance" and had "funeral solemnity," revealed the conspiracy to Newman and claimed that it was true and that Newman had the "patriotic duty to disseminate" it.

Next came Trudeau, "rolling out the word in his trademark serpentine inflection," who, exasperated by Newman's skepticism, confirmed the veracity of the story and said that the "plot to overthrow the government [was] real." The publisher of *The Toronto Star*, Beland Honderich, who was clearly in the Lalonde-Trudeau loop, personally then saw to it that the false story was circulated. Little doubt remains now that the publisher, the prime minister, and his chief political advisor knowingly lied, just as Marchand had knowingly lied earlier to members of Parliament in the House of Commons. What's more, both the "hawk" and the "serpent"— Newman's words—warned Newman that they would not hesitate to lie again and would deny that they had ever discussed the "conspiracy" with him. The "serpent" himself ended up committing the ultimate treachery by publicly and formally describing as "rumours and unconfirmed specula-tions" what he had sworn to Newman to be the "true" and "real."

◆

October 22, 1970: Rumours of war were being passed around Ottawa like after-dinner mints. Christina and I were attending a drawn-out cocktail party at the home of Trade minister Jean-Luc Pépin, a prime target of the Front de Libération du Québec since he was one of the province's most outspoken federalists. In his professorial way, Pépin was going on about the mayhem raging in his home province. "Revolutions are all the same," he was saying, though most of his guests were too nervous to listen. "Acts against the old order are invariably preceded by the disintegration of inward allegiances. The images of kings topple before their thrones."

"Well, yeah, I suppose—but what about Mike, here?" asked John Munro, one of Trudeau's better ministers, voicing the concern we were all feeling. Mike was an army private from Bell Island, in Conception Bay, Newfoundland, who had been assigned to guard the Pépins' household against the forces of evil stalking the trimmed hedges of Rockcliffe.

It was Day 17 of the FLQ's war against Canada and our first line of defence was Trooper Mike, who stumbled occasionally as he alternated between alcoholic hiccups and puzzled glances into the darkness beyond the living-room window. It was raining and Pépin, a fatherly type, had invited the soldier into the house to warm up and have a hot toddy or two. After asking our host to "Cut de sweet stuff, gimme de rum," our Screech Commando was feeling no pain. He was stomping around the living room, haphazardly aiming his loaded Isuzu or whatever it was, and we were positioning ourselves near pieces of furniture to duck behind. "I's de boy to squash dem crazy Frogs," he volunteered, which caught the attention of Jean-Luc, among others. When conversation stopped, he took this as a signal to fill up his ten minutes of fame with Newfie humour.

"De boys up in Gander," he confided, "want Quebec to separate, just so's we kin drive to Toronto in half the time." He accompanied the punchline with an emphatic wave of his James Bond-ish automatic rifle. It was a test. If we laughed too hard, he might think we were laughing at him and get mad. If we didn't, he would tell another joke. Somebody saved the situation by turning up the television set just as Montreal's police chief came on, looking sweaty and dishevelled.

"We're raiding blind," he confessed. "We've run out of leads." For some silly reason I kept repeating to myself Social Credit leader Bob

Thompson's recent malapropism: "If this thing starts to snowball, it will catch fire right across the country." The snowball had become an avalanche. Canada was in a state of unhinged frenzy. The mantra of TV news directors ("If it bleeds, it leads") had become the national script: the whole damn country was bleeding.

Someone changed the television channel to catch the CBC national evening news and called for quiet. The stern voice of Knowlton Nash filled the room, attempting to strike a tone somewhere between authoritative and calm, barely disguising his underlying panic. A communiqué from the Front de Libération du Québec claimed that two more kidnappings were under way. The Canadian army, swarming over Montreal in full force and battle dress, had turned the city into an armed camp. Another forty Montrealers, we learned, had been rounded up and jailed. The Commons was raucously debating the risk posed by unnamed collaborators coming to the aid of unindicted conspirators. It was Canada's first experience with domestic terrorism. We felt spooked and betrayed. Didn't these unshaven revolutionaries realize this was Canada, for goodness sake? We don't do revolutions. The tumult was deafening, but none of us knew how much of what we were hearing was real and how much was hysteria. All we knew was that it was too much to absorb.

Seventeen days had passed since British trade commissioner James Cross had been kidnapped by the FLQ, the first such political crime in Canadian history. It was twelve days since Quebec Labour minister Pierre Laporte had been snatched by another cell of the FLQ from the lawn of his home in suburban St. Lambert, while playing touch football with his sons. It was nine days since Pierre Trudeau had assured his place in history and in the hearts of Canadian federalists: when asked how far he would go to defeat the FLQ, even at the cost of their civil rights, he'd shot back, "Just watch me!" His cheeky defiance was for show; his brute strength was for real. But watch him we did, to the exclusion of all else.

It was seven days since, at the urgent behest of Quebec premier Robert Bourassa and Montreal mayor Jean Drapeau, seven battalions of Canadian soldiers had rolled into the city to re-establish the rule of law. It was six days since Jean Marchand, the Trudeau government's senior Quebec minister, had warned a frightened Parliament that the FLQ had three thousand trained members, with machine guns, bombs, and dynamite, ready to blow up downtown Montreal. "They have infiltrated every strategic position, every place where important decisions are taken," he warned. It was a week since the prime minister had invoked the War Measures Act, never before enacted in peacetime. By noon on October 16, some 465 men and women suspected of being friendly to the FLQ had been arrested without warrants or charges. It was five days since the corpse of Pierre Laporte, strangled with the chain of his own crucifix, had been found dead, stuffed into the trunk of a green Chevy abandoned in a parking lot at the St. Hubert airport. Quebec justice minister Jérôme Choquette had labelled the insurrection "a pre-revolutionary situation." With events escalated into the surreal it was difficult to believe that Canada wasn't heading for anarchy, or worse.

"Look at those eyes," I had remarked to Christina as we'd watched Trudeau's address to the nation, invoking the War Measures Act. "They're as barren as potholes." I could see her eyes gazing upward at hearing yet another one of my ditzy metaphors. She knew I would soon be rhapsodizing about his skull-formed face and his resemblance to a Buddhist monk in mufti.

Watching him declare a state of civil war, which he called an "apprehended insurrection," I was remembering the Trudeau I had seen in action two years previously. It was on June 24, only hours before the 1968 election, at Montreal's Lafontaine Park. The once-quiet Quebec revolution was gathering violent momentum. Trudeau was on the reviewing stand for the annual St. Jean Baptiste parade when furious protestors suddenly rushed toward him, shouting obscenities, hurling rocks and bottles. He stood his ground, the definition of grace under pressure, angrily waving off would-be bodyguards trying to shield him while the dignitaries who minutes before had surrounded him scattered for cover. The night was lit by a burning police car (twelve were overturned); beside me a cop on horseback reared up, preparing to charge back into the shrieking mob. "C'est une garce!" ("It's a bitch!") he said to no one in particular, then rode off, indiscriminately beating the rioters with his truncheon.

Claude Ryan was there that night, a gaunt, lonely figure in his light-grey windbreaker and battered fedora. "Have you ever seen anything like this?" I asked him.

"Not here," he said. "We had some hard times during the conscription crisis but nothing, nothing like this. You can not subdue revolutionary fervour with force. *C'est les situations sociales et économiques qui alimentent l'activité terroriste.* Social ills cause terrorist acts."

Back at the Pépins' we were preparing to leave when somebody told me I was on the FLQ's assassination list. "But don't worry:" He winked. "You're way behind Paul Desmarais and they'll never get him." Since I had briefly been a Catholic, I crossed myself. You never know.[2] Christina and I were the first to leave the party: The last time we saw Mike, the warrior from the Rock, he had been sent out into the rain and was carefully drawing a bead on the moon, laughing softly to himself.

The following day, we were urgently summoned to the East Block office of Marc Lalonde, the PM's principal secretary. Lalonde was as tough as nine generations of scrub farming on Île Perrot, off the southwestern tip of île de Montréal, could make him. "I'm a Norman farmer:" he loved to say. "It's like being from Missouri." He had come up through the militant Action Catholique movement, understood his people, and was Trudeau's closest adviser. We had known him since he'd first come to Ottawa under Pearson and admired his appreciation of Quebec politics, which was both visceral and cerebral. We trusted him. Thin, bald, hawk-like in appearance, he bade us sit across his messy desk from him. He smiled with funereal solemnity, in a way that underscored that this was no smiling matter, then proceeded to give us his grim reading of the deteriorating situation.

"Peter, Christina," he began, "I have called you here to discuss a matter of the utmost seriousness, but first I must warn you that I will deny this conversation ever took place."

We looked at each other and nodded. Reassured, Lalonde continued. "We believe that a group of prominent Québécois is plotting to replace the province's duly elected government," he said gravely. "The conspirators include René Lévesque, Jacques Parizeau, Marcel Pepin, and Claude Ryan. This move toward a parallel power must be stopped." He let the magnitude of the thought sink in for a moment.

"Not Ryan," Christina and I chimed in unison. "He is a man of conscience, dedicated to collective survival, not personal power. Besides,

---

2. (Newman's original footnote.) My name was indeed on the FLQ list when it was published. At the time, Paul Desmarais, chairman of Power Corporation, the largest agglomeration of private economic power in French Canada, was hunting pheasant on Île aux Ruaux in the St. Lawrence. The feds escorted him to safety aboard a landing craft manned by troops from Quebec City.

how do you know so much about the plot's members, their plans and intentions?"

"Because we know the ringleaders," he replied coolly. "We have been looking over their shoulders, you might say."

"Why are you telling us this? What do you expect us to do with such speculative information?" Christina demanded.

That brought him up short. "There is nothing speculative about this. It is true. I would surmise . . . that is to say . . . it would be prudent if certain individuals—certain individuals in the media—were made aware of the whole story . . ."

He looked up from his desk and flashed his sweetest smile, then repeated, "Of course, I cannot officially confirm anything for you."

Lalonde went on for most of an hour, trying not only to relieve our doubts but also hinting that it was our patriotic duty to disseminate news of this alarming development. We had known one another long enough that I could tell him he was full of it without calling him a liar, and I did so now, adding that I would give no credence to such a bizarre theory unless it was confirmed by Trudeau himself. "Not a problem," he answered right back. "He will call you. Where are you staying?"

Lalonde said *adieu*, closed his eyes, hunched over, and, with the seriousness of Galileo defending his theory of the universe, mumbled, "Pray for us." Chris and I looked at one another in disbelief. Our host was not impressed. "I don't suppose you people pray, anyway," he snorted, excommunicating us on the spot, as wormy Ontario Anglo Saxon Protestants, or in my case, a reasonable facsimile thereof.

We were barely back in our hotel room when the phone rang. It was Trudeau. With the insurrection yet to be apprehended, I hadn't really expected that the PM would bother taking the time to phone out-of-town journalists.

"Peter?" he asked, rolling out the word in his trademark serpentine inflection. "Marc tells me that he had a very interesting conversation with you and Christina today. And how is your lovely wife?"

"She's fine," I replied, respectfully, though trying to keep a cool distance. "But she is confused and worried, as I am. Look, Pierre, you know what Marc told us. Is there anything to it? You once explained to me that revolutions may devour humanity, but it's tyranny that generates violence. Claude Ryan might be part of the revolution, but he's no tyrant."

"Tyranny has many agents," he replied, sounding annoyingly Pierre-like.

There was a long pause, as though he was conferring with someone, or reading a note. "Yes, Peter," he replied at last. "I can confirm it. There is a conspiracy afoot. The ringleaders are Lévesque. Parizeau, and Ryan, among others. This move toward a parallel power must be stopped."

"Even if Ryan is organizing a political group," I objected, "it's only to give Bourassa some backbone. It hardly amounts to *un coup de main* . . ."

"Unelected power is not moved by benign motives," he replied with an edge of annoyance. I realized his patience was running out. "Look," he said, sounding exasperated, "what Marc told you and Christina is true: the plot to overthrow the government is real."

"With respect, how can you be so sure?"

"I acted on information I've been accumulating since I was three years old."

In other words, "Buzz off *Anglais*."

He added that I couldn't quote him or even mention that we had talked. (I am doing so now, for the first time, long after his death.)

"But Pierre, perhaps in this case what you lacked in evidence, you have made up from conviction . . ."

The line had gone dead.

I turned to Christina, waiting with a worried look of expectation. "Pierre says it's true," I told her. "It's a coup."

She fell back into the sofa and shook her head incredulously. "This is Canada," she said. "I can't believe it. This is Canada."

We decided that while we weren't really sure what was true and what was convenient for the government to spread, either way we had the story of the decade.

Ottawa's social event of the year was scheduled for the following evening: the annual reception given by the super-bureaucrats Bernard and Sylvia Ostry at Five Oaks, their splendid mansion on the Quebec-Ontario border, the epicentre of Ottawa's power structure. Their living room was where decisions were debated, influence paraded, special favours refused and granted. Christina and I had become regulars at these shindigs. We had been there when Trudeau was justice minister and allowed a visiting rock group to light up their weird cigarettes, though he didn't join them. But this gathering was different. Half the Trudeau Cabinet ministers were present, as were the key (as opposed to just the senior) deputies, earnestly whispering to one another in the corners of the large reception room, all the while watched over by their armed guards. I spotted a sobered-up Mike from the Pépin household and gave him a playful poke in the shoulder. He didn't shoot me.

The gossip was mainly about "Bou-Bou," the favoured nickname for Premier Robert Bourassa, who, it was said, had lost his halls and was at permanent panic stations, barricaded into the twentieth floor of Montreal's Queen Elizabeth Hotel. But his predicament was overtaken by the rumour of a "provisional government plot," which nobody would confirm or deny but which was certainly floating out there as the conversational truffle of the hour. I distinctly remember Alex Pelletier, a film producer and the wife of Gérard Pelletier, Trudeau's secretary of state, telling anybody who would listen, "Claude Ryan is out to take over the government, and has to be put down?" It was stated as a fact instead of conjecture, but few were buying her version of events. Christina and I realized that our scoop was more perishable than we had imagined.

What many in this stodgy gathering wanted to hear was that their boy Pierre was about to put down those Gallic rebs with their dirty beards and raised fists, while at the same time protecting the realm from windy intellectuals like Claude Ryan and the terror of his convoluted editorials. Paul Desmarais was there, looking unperturbed, but packing a revolver, it was whispered. (…)

Just then an executive assistant I knew ran out of the house to announce he had been told "on good authority by one of BouBou's bully boys" that this weekend five hundred of Quebec's leading citizens would be assassinated. "But don't tell anybody!" he called over his shoulder, and moved on.

We returned indoors where the armed troopers were busy examining Bernard Ostry's vintage books and vintage liquor. Christina and I had to keep quiet about our recent conversations but realized it was time to skedaddle.

By Sunday noon, I was back in my editor's chair at the *Toronto Star* and had contacted Robert McKenzie, our experienced Quebec City correspondent, to check out the story. He talked to Ryan and reported back on Claude's—and his own—disbelief that we would even consider publishing such a bizarre rumour. Our Montreal editor agreed, but added that I should listen to what the mayor was going to say when the ballots had been counted. I had forgotten that this was the day of the Montreal municipal election. Jean Drapeau won by a margin of 92 per cent. At his victory press conference he surprised his supporters (and me) by thanking them for "resisting, not only known revolutionary attacks but also attempts to set up a provisional government that was to preside over the transfer of constitutional powers to a revolutionary regime."

Suddenly, I had confirmation of the story, not only from the prime minister of Canada in private, but from the mayor of Montreal in public.

I still wasn't convinced. I wrote the article very gingerly, emphasizing that "the factor which finally drove the Trudeau Government to invoke the War Measures Act was that they had become convinced a plan existed to replace the Government"—that it was the Trudeau adminis- tration (not *moi*) which "believed that a group of influential Quebeckers had set out to supplant the legitimately elected provincial administra- tion." In other words, I took care to make it clear that I was reporting what I had been told, without subscribing to the notion myself. This was a distinction quickly lost on my peers, my colleagues, and my readers. They either wanted to believe that the provisional government story was true, or that I was deliberately spreading a falsehood, or both.

I mentioned no names of suspected conspirators, since I couldn't bring myself to believe that Claude Ryan could align himself with such an inflammatory abuse of power. I knew him well. We had connected the moment we met, several years earlier. Since then I had often called on him at the cobblestoned end of Rue Notre Dame and spent many enjoyable hours discussing Quebec's prospects in his bare cell of an office. There was no soft side to him. His face had the aesthetic strength of wisdom born through suffering, with hooded eyes and a nose sharp- ened as if to probe his visitors' intentions. He was the rational voice and resident saint of Quebec's Quiet Revolution, and I implicitly trusted him. Not that long ago, we had spent a day in my *Star* office (where I was now completing my article) drafting the manifesto of the Committee for an Independent Canada, which he would later co-chair. The more often we talked, the more I admired and trusted him.

I phoned Ryan and left a message: "Claude, you probably know the story I've heard. I'm writing it. Can you give me an unqualified denial?"

Beland Honderich had meanwhile come into the office. The decision as to whether or not to publish my piece would be made at the very top. The publisher had in turn brought in Jake Howard, a leading Toronto libel lawyer (who happened to have been my training officer aboard HMCS *Iroquois*). I was in Bee's office when he telephoned Ryan: "Claude, what do you say about this story being circulated about you?"

"For God's sake, Bee, tell me what things you are going to circulate." Ryan was becoming increasingly agitated. "We're not in Hitler's Germany, you know. We're in Canada."

Honderich summarized my story; then added: "We are going to publish the story, but with no names in it."

"That's not my concept of journalism," Ryan replied harshly. "As a matter of principle, I repudiate this kind of journalism, very, very strongly."

When I asked Howard whether I could include Ryan's denial, which I had by then received on my message machine, he pointed out that the mention of any name might leave us open to accusations of sedition, against which we would have no defence. I agreed to publish the six-paragraph piece, but Honderich ruled that it should remain anonymous, because so many people had worked on it, so it was slugged "From Our Ottawa Bureau." I was wrong not to insist that it go out under my name. Our Ottawa Bureau journalists quickly denied authorship, telling callers that I had been in town asking questions and that it was undoubtedly my handiwork.

The story took on a life of its own. To his surprise, *Telegram* columnist Douglas Fisher found "an unidentified but reliable" source who confirmed my story, and went even further: "Why don't you have Sonic faith in us? Surely you must know we wouldn't have taken such an extraordinary step unless the threat was very, very serious. We learned from unimpeachable sources that such a takeover was planned. Really big people involved. Trudeau is the last man in this country to panic. We moved on the War Measures Act because it was that or chaos." Half a dozen other papers published my version of events; even the reliable Pierre O'Neil of *La Presse* labelled the facts as "*incroyables mais apparemment vrais*" ("unbelievable but apparently true"). Most other reporters decided to kill the messenger. I had seldom been the target of such malice. The *Telegram* labelled my story "grotesque"; the CBC's Larry Zolf called it a "plant"; the *Globe* ridiculed my "fantasy born of hysteria"; and the *Montreal Gazette* pointed out that it "defied belief."

What I didn't know at the time was that all of these critiques were entirely accurate.

I later learned that the original source of the provisional government rumour was none other than Claude Ryan himself. On October 11, the day after Laporte's kidnapping, Robert Bourassa had begun to lose his grip on events and on his ability to respond. Ryan called an emergency editorial board meeting to discuss ways of strengthening the premier's backbone and his government's clout. The controversial alternative-government option had indeed been discussed and just as quickly rejected—all within the context, not of setting up a parallel government, but of enlisting community leaders to strengthen Bourassa's slipping hold on power. During a conversation the same day with Lucien Saulnier, chairman of the Montreal's executive committee, Ryan mentioned the idea of a provisional government as a last resort if the kidnappings continued and Bourassa's deteriorating control of the situation presented a danger to the rule of law. "Then," he said, "and only then, there surely wouldn't be much choice but to set up a unity government, made up of the best elements." He feared that unless order was restored, Ottawa might place Quebec under some form of stewardship, which he wouldn't put past Trudeau. Saulnier passed Ryan's comments on to Lalonde, who reported them to the PM. Somewhere along the line, *Le Devoir*'s editorial board blue-sky discussion was transformed into an intended coup.

Eight days after I first heard it the story was finally shot down by its most illustrious source: Pierre Elliott Trudeau. At an Ottawa press conference on October 31, he casually confirmed that the feds had indeed been "looking over the shoulders" of the "conspirators" who were intending to form a "provisional regime." He went on to remark that there had never been any hard evidence that the group was going to carry out its intentions. He dismissed my report in the *Star* as being based on "rumours and unconfirmed speculations" and later told the House of Commons: "It has not been the government but rather the Opposition and the Press Gallery that have been launching these rumours."

Zut alors! They were his rumours. Not mine.

I felt angry and cheated by Trudeau's revisionist version of events. I hadn't been in Ottawa for a dozen years without becoming inured to the fact that prime ministers lie; it comes with the territory. I had made my reputation writing stories about political chicanery but had seldom before become its victim.

Then the penny began to drop. If the prime minister could reverse himself so casually, then the entire scenario had been a meticulously concocted lie, with Christina and me the unwitting accomplices in the feds' attempt to discredit Ryan. There had never been a plot, just Claude's musings during a gut-wrenching crisis. But when we had talked to Lalonde and Trudeau on October 23, they had not differentiated between what they knew to be true and what they wished to be true. *Le Devoir*'s publisher had always been a threat to their vision of the province as a federal preserve, for Ryan was Quebec's voice of conscience, a role that Trudeau could no longer claim as exclusively his own.

In the public's mind, the imposition of the War Measures Act and the call-up of troops to restore order in Montreal and guard Ottawa's politicians were cause and effect of the same phenomenon. In fact, there was no connection. On October 16 when Drapeau and Bourassa demanded the presence of Canada's armed forces in the city and the province, they were merely citing relevant provisions of the National Defence Act, which requires Ottawa to grant such requests almost automatically. In retrospect, Trudeau might have overreacted by calling up 7,500 soldiers to combat the violent acts of a dozen revolutionaries. The armed might mobilized by the prime minister was awesome. (In those days, Canada could still assemble an army with meaningful fire-power.) To put the call-up in perspective: seven battalions were assigned to Montreal, while nine battalions were involved in the 1942 raid on Dieppe, among the largest of Canada's armed interventions during the Second World War.

Another link usually cited in any reconstruction of the crisis was that the imposition of the War Measures Act was a desperate response to Laporte's execution. Not so. That legal escalation was formally requested by Quebec's premier at 3:00 a.m. on Friday, October 16, and granted an hour later. Laporte's assassination was announced by the FLQ a full twenty-four hours after that, and his body was not found until late the following day.

The first hint that all was not what it seemed here was an obscure paragraph in an obscure memoir by Donald Jamieson, the Trudeau government's Transport minister. He interpreted Trudeau's headlong rush into proclaiming the War Measures Act not as a specific measure to combat any "apprehended insurrection" (which is what the act cited as the only appropriate *casus belli*) but rather as a political move to shore up the prime minister's obsession with defanging Quebec's separatists. Unlike the troop mobilization, Ottawa did not have to accede to the province's request for imposition of the War Measures Act. Several senior ministers, including Jamieson, John Turner, Joe Greene, and Mitchell Sharp, were strongly opposed, since the act had never been activated except in wartime, and in this case there existed lesser, equally effective options. Jamieson suggested that a Cabinet committee be struck to demonstrate why the draconian measure had been necessary. To his surprise, Trudeau did not take up the idea. "Subsequent events made his reason for non-response very plain," Jamieson wrote. "It was his growing awareness that very little in the way of concrete evidence was going to turn up. I and others in cabinet were quite uneasy over this turn of events." He predicted that critics of the measure would realize "we had acted for political reasons or from something less than simon-pure motives." Exactly.

Guided by York University historian Reg Whitaker, I delved into the documents available under the Freedom of Information Act and found the minutes of a confidential briefing, presented to Trudeau two days before the invocation of the War Measures Act. Unlike most police officers faced by persistent politicians, William Higgitt, the commissioner of the Royal Canadian Mounted Police, proved to be very tough, very precise, and equally persistent. Asked repeatedly how the provision would assist his police work, Higgitt's studied reply was recorded in the meeting's unemotional minutes: "The Commissioner said he saw no necessary action being prevented by existing laws. He said that a broad sweep and preventive detention of suspects was not likely to lead to the abductors and that he could therefore not recommend the use of special powers." For good measure, Higgitt warned that Quebec "wanted action for the sake of action" and that this "ought not to be allowed to overrule calmer reaction at the federal level." Higgitt was called back to brief the Cabinet after the feds' dragnet had haphazardly imprisoned 465 suspects. He told the ministers that this draconian measure had produced "nothing of consequence." Near the end of this second briefing (which Trudeau did not attend) the RCMP commissioner was asked bluntly whether he had evidence that any kind of insurrection was being planned. "Not really," he replied, "there is no such evidence." Shortly afterwards, during a private session with British Foreign secretary Sir Alec Douglas-Home in London, External Affairs secretary Mitchell Sharp confessed that, indeed, "there was no evidence of an extensive and coordinated FLQ conspiracy."

Out of this and other evidence, I easily conclude that Trudeau invoked the War Measures Act as a partisan weapon to intimidate Quebec's separatists for his own political purposes. The only apprehended insurrection the PM had going for him was the puny parallel government rumour in my story, which was not an insurrection, nor had it been apprehended, since it never got started.

What most likely happened followed the merry-go-round mentality of any Ottawa conspiracy when its members are attempting to justify, or hide, dubious actions. Lalonde heard from Saulnier that Ryan had been musing about a provisional government. Somewhere along the line, the version was torqued out of all recognition. The feds had to find a way of disseminating the story to their power network, which in turn would persuade the country's mainstream media to believe it was true. The fact that the information was disseminated only within a closed loop gave the story much higher cachet. First they got the mayor of Montreal believing it, then the Cabinet, then the Newmans and other chosen mouthpieces, and soon, enough of "the people who matter" were spreading the rumour as if it were true – even if its originators didn't entirely believe it.[3]

As the disturbing facts of that episode unfolded, I became determined that I would treat Lucky Pierre as just another political gunslinger, and not as the phantom of my opera. The gunslinger image seemed apt. He might just as easily have been one of those fabled cowboys who flourished briefly across the American West in the mid-nineteenth century. The code they lived by found resonance in Trudeau's politics, because the mark of the gunslingers was their courage of the early morning and the rawhide toughness of their quest. But they also viewed their lives as a series of throwaway gestures, as did Pierre. Like the best of the vintage frontier vigilantes, he was a loner who risked everything in the shootouts of electoral politics. But unlike most of the gunslingers, he did not end his career being scraped off some bar-room floor. Instead he turned himself into a self-appointed posse of one in charge of reforming Canada's constitution—and no man (or Supreme Court) could stand in his way.

3. (Newman's original note.) How long this version of events survived was illustrated on February 10, 2004, when Claude Ryan died of stomach cancer, and in his *Globe and Mail* obituary Rhéal Séguin described the *Le Devoir* publisher's role in the FLQ crisis of 1970 this way: "At one point, fearing that the Bourassa regime was on the verge of collapsing, Ryan and others secretly set up a parallel government."

Trudeau minister Jean Marchand claimed the FLQ had some 3000 well-trained terrorists armed to the teeth. (Cartoon by Aislin first published in MacLean's in October 1970. Reprinted courtesy of Aislin (Terry Mosher).)

6

NOBODY WAS LEFT UNSCATHED

6.1 In Quebec

"Everybody was up for grabs."

Nick Auf der MAUR

◆

EDITORS' NOTES

No less than three thousand people packed into the church to attend Nick Auf der Maur's funeral in April 1998. For thirty years, Nick Auf der Maur had earned a reputation in diverse political and social circles in Montreal. Among his many friends were writer Mordecai Richler and cartoonist Terry Mosher (Aislin). He was known to the general public as a journalist with the *Gazette*, the defunct *Montreal Star,* and on CBC, but also as a municipal politician, having been elected to the Montreal City Council four times (1974, 1978, 1982, 1986). He was an attractive and eclectic public figure as a fellow *Gazette* columnist pointed out: "Nick's funeral was a fitting last call, a huge gathering of the clan that was almost as eclectic as the people who had drunk with him. There were out-of-town journalists, actors and rock stars, ex-mayors and politicians, pin-striped lawyers, cabdrivers, plumbers, priests, and panhandlers. They were rich and poor, federalist and separatist, left wing and right wing."[1]

Though he was a political boulevardier, he had also been a man of conviction and commitment. Nick Auf der Maur was born in 1942 to a Swiss immigrant family in a working-class neighbourhood of Montreal. He became interested in politics during the first years of the Quiet Revolution when Quebec nationalized electricity and he passionately followed what René Lévesque did and said. "I became a fan," he said of René Lévesque when the former Quebec premier died. He then added: "It was inevitable that those of our generation who got their first taste of political passion

---

1. "The Last Call was for 3,000." In *Nick, A Montreal Life*, Edited by Dave Bist; Introduction by Mordecai Richler; caricatures by Aislin, Véhicule Press, Montreal, 1998, p. 47.

and ideals from the lips and mind of René Lévesque would be, a few years down the line, the foot soldiers of all the changes that were to come."[2]

That political spark led him to the left towards the end of the 1960s. He gained a solid reputation as editor of *The Last Post*, a committed left-wing publication which, like others in North America, opposed capitalism, imperialism, and the Vietnam war, and supported the Third World. He was an English-speaking Montrealer very well linked with the rest of the Quebec people. In 1972, in the preface to a Last Post publication, Robert Chodos wrote: "There is no English-language journalist in Montreal who has as many contacts at all levels from the government to the FLQ, is as knowledgeable about events in Quebec or can write as cogently about them as Nick Auf der Maur, and *The Last Post* has been very fortunate to have him as its Quebec editor."[3]

October 1970 and the war measures came along. Was it because of his left-wing politics, his hostility towards Montreal Mayor Jean Drapeau, or his growing notoriety—he was already hosting a CBC television program? Whatever the reason, his name turned up on an RCMP list and that landed him in prison for several days. As a journalist, he very naturally told the story of his arrest and his time in jail in an article in *The Last Post* in November 1970.[4] We have chosen that text because it was written originally in English, but also because it appears to have been forgotten by those who published an anthology of his writings after his death entitled *Nick, A Montreal Life*.

Historian Desmond Morton discusses the 1970 war measures in his history of the Canadian Army and points out that Trudeau was not out to get the members of the two FLQ cells, but rather the "coffee table revolutionaries," the "affluent dilettantes of revolutionary violence," those who he had warned a year earlier in his speech "Fini les folies!" (See Morton's observations in Chapter 8.) For those who had just been given free reins to lock people up under the war measures, Nick Auf der Maur was the ideal target simply because of his notoriety. The fact that he was an English-speaking Quebecer made him even more interesting. What better way to show English Montrealers the price they would have to pay for their solidarity with the new Quebec that was developing?

◆

2. "An Extraordinary man shaped exciting times," in *Nick A Montreal Life*, pp. 206-207.

3. *Quebec; A Chronicle 1968-1972, A Last Post Special*, edited by Nick Auf der Maur and Robert Chodos; with a Postscript by Yvon Charbonneau, Louis Laberge and Marcel Pepin, James Lewis and Samuel Publishers, Toronto, 1972, p. 2.

4. Nick Auf der Maur, "Memoirs of a prisoner of war," *The Last Post*, Vol. 1, No. 5, p. 15.

The day after the War Measures Act was passed, a friend came up to me and said he had seen my place being raided on TV. "What?" (That's the term most people used to react to fresh developments throughout the whole affair.) It turned out it wasn't my place, but the apartment where I used to live. I sublet it to a group of South Vietnamese students and they were all arrested. It was hard to figure out, because they had little or nothing to do with local politics. But from the beginning, the arrests had seemed indiscriminate.

Over the weekend, I ran into all sorts of people. Many of them were very apprehensive. "They can hold you for 90 days… incommunicado." Old tales of beatings by the police were resurrected. The arrests kept up.

It took a while to sink in, but it did. Everybody was up for grabs. The disturbing thing was that not too many people seemed disturbed. "If you have nothing to hide, a clear conscience, then you have nothing to worry about," was the usual reaction from a lot of people, "It's only aimed at the FLQ." Trouble is, the police were armed with a blunderbuss.

The city scene was filled with police cars racing to and fro, running red lights. Truckloads of soldiers lurched through the streets. One was reminded of American generals in Vietnam: "Just give us the tools, and we'll do the job."

There they were: the RCMP, the Quebec Police Force, the city of Montreal police, the army regiments and paratroopers from weird, faraway bases; the grim, but contented-faced plainclothesmen. The city was completely open to them. Arrest who you like, stop who you like, search and raid wherever you like. They were, as one wag commented, as happy as pigs in a puddle.

But, like the generals in Vietnam, they didn't get anywhere. And this worried more people. The police will get angry, arrest more people, beat them up. More and more people were staying at the homes of acquaintances.

Pierre Laporte was killed over the weekend. And there was less publicly voiced opposition to the War Measures Act. For a lot of people, that kind of talk made one sound suspiciously like a sympathizer of the FLQ. One of English Montreal's most popular radio commentators, Rod Dewar, a liberal, was yanked off the air for his views.

Tuesday night, we were sitting in a tavern. A friend came over and said my apartment was raided. I phoned up my landlord, who lives in the building. He told me they arrived about 7 o'clock, a dozen or so in and out of uniform. They searched the entire building, including his living quarters and antique store. The girl who lives downstairs has a big dog which is trained to growl at strangers. They pulled out guns and were going to shoot the animal to effect an undisturbed search. The landlord was advised they had this right, since the owner wasn't there to keep the dog at bay. Cooler heads prevailed and they decided to forget that apartment and search mine. They seized my passport and a few papers.

The next day at work, just as I was about to go to lunch, I received a telephone call from Cpl. Dumas of the RCMP: "We'd like to talk to you. We'll meet you in five minutes at the corner of Stanley and Dorchester."

"Are you going to arrest me?" I inquired.

"We'll see. We just want to talk to you."

"Can't it wait until after lunch… I've made arrangements. .

There was a muffled noise, then the voice: "Meet us in five minutes, we'd like to talk to you."

"You're going to arrest me," I said.

"We just want to talk to you."

I discussed it with my colleagues. None of the previously arrested people had been released yet. The police can hold you a long time with no reason.

What the hell, I thought, I have nothing to hide, my conscience is clear. So, along with two colleagues for witnesses, I went to meet them a block away.

Their car was in a parking lot and they were smiling, these two detectives from the RCMP. They told my friends everything was OK and they could go, they just wanted to talk to me privately in the car.

We drove a half a block and parked.

"You went to the Lemieux press conferences Who did you see?"

They acted friendly and slightly apologetic. They wanted to know if I recognized Paul Rose and Marc Carbonneau or anybody else at the press conferences. I didn't.

What about the FLQ, or the cells? Nothing that hasn't been printed. "I don't know anything," I said. "We believe you," one of them chuckled.

Well, the two men in the front seat drew closer, what about "foreign organizations?"

"Are you kidding," I replied, telling them I thought all that stuff, like *Montreal Gazette* stories about Cuban waiters at Expo '67 spending weekends training guerrillas in the Laurentians, was a lot of hooey.

"How about the Black Panthers?" I told them I met one, from California, on a visit here and he barely knew some people spoke French in Quebec.

They laughed and announced they "had" to take me to Parthenais street, the provincial police headquarters. I asked them who decides who should be arrested. "Higherups," was the answer.

At Parthenais Street, they drove into the wrong driveway. I guessed these two hadn't brought many people here before me. We were directed towards the basement garage. Combat-equipped soldiers searched the trunk of the car before we were let in.

In the basement we waited for an elevator. A huge barred gate appeared to block off the area. Right beside the elevator, there were two cells with steel doors and small glass windows. They were brightly lit. I looked inside. There was nothing. They were the size of closets, two feet wide and three and a half feet long. It looked ominous.

My two RCMP friends took me up to the fourth floor where they left me to be checked in. I was led down a narrow corridor, through a series of electronically operated barred gates. We arrived at a cell with a steel door and a small glass window. Inside, it was four paces long and two and a half paces wide, with a single steel bunk, basin and toilet bowl. (…)

Here I was, I thought, I hadn't done anything and didn't know a damn thing about "an apprehended insurrection." What are they doing with me… I wasn't particularly worried, since I assumed everything would be sorted out. It was quiet where I was, so all I could do was think. It kept recurring to me that I was a political prisoner. It doesn't matter that I've done nothing. That train of thought, which could be depressing, was interrupted an hour later by voices. I called out:

"Hello, how long have you been here?"

Several voices shouted out, "il y a un nouveau", there's a new guy. It turned out I was in the second cell of a long row. I couldn't see anybody but we could talk. They asked my name. I told them. A whole bunch of familiar voices rang out: "Hi Nick… what are you doing here?"

I seemed to be in the company of all the "grosses légumes." Vallières, Gagnon, Lemieux, Michel Chartrand. The closest one to me was Reggie Chartrand. Greetings were short. They were hungry for news of the outside. They told me they only knew of Laporte's death when they noticed flags flying at half-mast.

We shouted back and forth. Everybody seemed to be in good spirits.

Supper was delivered to our cells. It was surprisingly good.

Unfortunately they didn't keep up the same standard throughout my stay.

After supper, I was taken to be fingerprinted and photographed.

In the evening, Reggie Chartrand did most of the talking. He was bitter that there weren't more protests on the outside against the War Measures Act. He was particularly displeased with the students.

"Ils fument du 'pot' et font rien. C'est des 'punks' avec diplomes."

I expected I was going to be put through all sorts of interrogation. But, according to the others, interrogation was only cursory, minimal. Aside from being kept in the cells all the time, everybody was fairly well treated… no rough stuff. You even got used to sleeping with the lights on all night. We were allowed to keep our cigarettes but had to call a guard for a light. They were always obliging.

The next morning, Thursday, nothing much happened except they allowed one guy out to take a shower. Later, they led a new prisoner in. I looked through the window and recognized him as he walked by. I shouted to him, but he couldn't see me.

When he was installed in his cell and the guards left, somebody asked him where he got arrested.

"At the University of Quebec," he answered, "I was teaching class. Two guys came in and took me out."

I decided that the two cops who arrested me didn't come up to my office not to save me embarrassment, as they intimated, but to avoid the appearances of police statism in respectable places. Universities, obviously, aren't respectable.

After lunch, a couple of guys, including Reggie Chartrand, were led away and never came back. A while later we noticed Reggie standing on the street across the way. Sanity, I thought, they'll soon be releasing me.

A guard came by and opened the door. This is it, I smiled. He just wanted my belt. A while later I was let out of the cell while a cleaner mopped the floor. I felt good just standing outside, in the corridor, all of 30 seconds. Clang.

Around 4:30 three other guys and myself were called and led out to where we were checked in. We felt good. One day, for me, everything is sorted out. They gave us our personal belongings back, counted out our money. I put my belt back on.

The four of us were put in an elevator which resembled a mobile cell, and brought up to the tenth floor. We went through the same checking-in process. I asked them what was going on. A guard said that the fourth floor was simply a detention centre, run by the police, and this was a real jail, run by prison authorities.

We were forced to undress as they thoroughly searched our clothing, our bodies and even our hair.

Our new home was located on the thirteenth floor, in cell block 13 AG. I was assigned cell number 2, which made me 13 AG 2 (thirteenth floor "à gauche"—to the left). The cell was slightly bigger, although a bit dank. After dinner, they let us out of our cells for a half-hour recreation period. The four of us, the new arrivals, shook hands with everyone else and said hello. Afterwards it was back into the cells. Up here, there was at least something to read. A quick inventory of the library produced: two copies of the Readers' Digest in French, one in English; one in Swedish and one in Dutch; two copies of Fortune; a 1968 issue of Time; and, peculiarly, a French-language magazine from Poland.

The makeup of the prisoners was pretty interesting. While there was a heavy, contingent of intellectual types, there were very few students: The prisoners represented a fairly general cross-section of Quebec society. A Canadian Ambassador's son occupied a cell down from me. His neighbor was a construction worker, assigned by his union to guard Charles Gagnon after his life had been threatened by some mysterious right-wing group. There were poets, union officials, workers, teachers, students, journalists.

In the evening, we chatted back and forth, not seeing each other. Somebody read one of those quotable quotes from the Readers' Digest: "When I was young, I used to think that socialism was the mathematics of justice; now I know it is the arithmetic of envy." The quote provoked much lively debate, consisting mostly of epithets and denunciations of brainwashing in the social-prison system. (…)

While in prison, no one talked about the FLQ, at least not in specific terms. Since we had absolutely no news of what was happening on the outside (we later learned the guards had instructions not to tell us anything) we were in a suspended, frozen state. Almost all the people I was with had been in since early Friday morning, when the War Measures Act was decreed, so I was a sought-after source for the latest developments.

My favorite story concerned The Gazette, my former employer. It seems that on that Friday, or perhaps it was the Friday before, a Gazette police reporter phoned the office from police headquarters. The police had staked out a small farmhouse outside Varennes, on the South Shore, where Cross was being held. "This could be it," he told his editor, "There might be a shoot-out, better get someone over there." He gave the exact location of the house. A half hour later he phoned back the office to give additional information. "Don't worry," the editor said, "we've got the whole situation under control... we've sent out a reporter and photographer in a helicopter... we'll swoop in, get pictures...

The reporter cried out, You fools, or something to that effect, it's a secret stakeout. The police are hidden. You'll give them away.

From descriptions I heard, complete panic broke out at *The Gazette*, something along the lines of Dr. Strangelove: "Bring back that plane!" The editors ran around in a frenzy, they just killed Cross, they were ruined.

During their first call to the Department of Transport at the airport, an official exclaimed: "Is this some kind of publicity stunt?" and hung up. Fortunately, for the *Gazette*'s collective nerves, they got through in the nick of time and radioed the helicopter back. Of course, in the end, the police tip was all wrong anyway.

That pleased them. So did the news that on the day the WMA was enacted, a radio station in Quebec City continuously played Pauline Julien songs (she was arrested) and Mikis Theodorakis music.

The next day, Friday, there was a variation in our routine. We were allowed out of our cells most of the afternoon. We played cards together and generally had a pleasant time.

In the evening everything changed, at least for me.

I was called for questioning shortly after supper. I was led down to the tenth floor, into a little office used for client-lawyer consultations. There was a detective from the RCMP and one from the Montreal city police. They didn't give their names.

The RCMP man had a three-page form which he filled in, asking me my mother's maiden name, schooling and all sorts of personal data.

Then he asked me things like why I went to Vallières' house. I told him (truthfully) that I'd never been to his house. They asked me about other people I knew, like Mario Bachand, who served time for the 1963 FLQ. He jumped bail a year and a half ago on a very involved charge which resulted after five policemen were discovered videotaping a private meeting being held in a school hall. The meeting and everything about it were legal but Bachand was charged with extortion and several other things when somebody else relieved the police of their tapes. He went to Cuba where he is now probably smoking cigars and cutting cane.

The questioning was almost conversational, with the RCMP man doing most of the talking. The other detective was writing something on a note pad.

At one point, he slid the pad over and asked me to write out the alphabet, first in capitals then in small letters. I obliged, all the time keeping up the talk with the other one. Then I was asked to write out a few sentences. I wrote: Now is the time for all good men to come to the aid of the party and the quick brown fox. Still talking to the other fellow, he asked me to sign what I wrote. I did.

Curiously, they never asked me about the current FLQ or if I knew anything about it.

I was brought back to my cell block. The other prisoners, some of whom still hadn't been questioned after a week, asked me what happened. I told them. Some of them reacted with horror when I told them I signed the things I wrote. "What else was on the paper?" they asked. "Was there any blank spaces for them to fill in something?"

Stupidly, I realized that maybe I had been had by one of the oldest tricks in the book. After recreation I went back to my cell saying "stupid, stupid, stupid."

Up until that point, despite the fact I knew better I always had a vague assumption that the police, if not the authorities, acted on good faith, that they were really only after people they thought guilty. Now I had a very different feeling. They're out to get everybody. They were probably under enormous pressure from the governments to produce results, and they were going to do it one way or another. The thought was depressing.

Lying down on my bunk, I recalled a discussion I had a few days earlier with some foreign journalists.

The foreign journalists seemed more worked up about the consequences than the home-grown variety. "If this happened in the States, all hell would break loose," said one. "This could never happen in Britain," added another over a beer. "What about the Bill of Rights?" somebody asked. He was incredulous when I told him we've only had one for five years of so. I threw in the fact that we've only had a national flag for a few years. For good measure, I said that the elections coming up in Montreal would be the first here with universal suffrage. Previously, only property-owners and water-tax payers could vote. I told them about the Padlock Law under Duplessis; when police could lock up an apartment or a building simply by declaring it was used for "Communist" purposes.

I told them a few things about Canada's economic situation, about the eighty per cent foreign control, about French-English relations and about a number of other things. As the discussion carried on, I realized that from a foreigner's point of view, the picture of Canada as a banana republic is easily made.

To add a little colour to this view I said: "Consider this: in 1942 Michel Chartrand was Jean Drapeau's campaign manager when he first ran for public office. Today Drapeau is Mayor of Montreal and Chartrand is in jail. In 1963, Pierre Elliott Trudeau personally selected Pierre Vallières as his successor to the editorship of the magazine Cité Libre. Today Trudeau is Prime Minister of Canada and Vallières is in jail. In 1967, René Lévesque drew up his thesis for a sovereign Quebec within a Canadian economic union. Most of the economic part of the thesis was written in Robert Bourassa's basement with his help on his typewriter. Today Bourassa is Premier of Quebec and they're going to try and drag Lévesque under with the FLQ."

Sitting in my jail cell, considering the War Measures Act, the police, the politicians, the situation and everything else, I started to think that maybe this is the crunch and we're all going to stay in jail for a long time as political prisoners. Considering the hysteria on the outside, this jail cell reasoning seemed pretty valid at that point. (...)

The processing took about an hour. During that time I talked with a middle-aged worker who belonged to a citizens' committee in one of Montreal's poorer areas. He had been arrested an hour after the WMA was decreed. The police broke down his door and took him away from his family. After eight days in jail, he thought he probably had lost his job.

The stupidest thing about it though, he said, is that they never asked him a single question.

"In the middle of the night."
John Cruickshank

◆

EDITORS' NOTES
"Tomorrow morning, preferably in the small hours, any one of you may be arrested," warned Pierre Trudeau in 1958, at a time when Maurice Duplessis was still solidly ensconced at the head of the Quebec government. He would use that image—one of the twentieth century's darkest—many times and for many years thereafter. In 1955, during a "friendly" conversation with poet and activist Gaston Miron, whom he hoped to convince of the necessity of dropping his dreams of independence, Trudeau thought he might intimidate Miron by alluding to arrests "in the middle of the night," as reported in the article below. Again in 1968 during the constitutional conference held in Ottawa, Pierre Trudeau, who had become minister of Justice, made a plea to Premier Daniel Johnson in favour of a charter of rights, reminding him that in Canada people could be apprehended "in the middle of the night and kept incommunicado for several days."[1] Then on October 14, 1970, within days of what some people have described as "his finest hour," he once again referred to that hour, this time in the House of Commons: "If urgent action is needed at some time *in the middle of the night*..."

What was for him but inoffensive rhetoric became harsh reality for an entire people. With the stroke of *his* pen, the War Measures Act was proclaimed and, of course, it was imposed as he had imagined, "in the middle of the night," at 4 a.m. exactly. The first arrests were made at 4:30 a.m., and by 8 a.m. two hundred and fifty people were detained. In the following days, the police searched thousands of homes "in the middle of the night." When Hugh Segal reflected on the "jack-boot approach" of Pierre Trudeau, Marc Lalonde, and the others in October 1970, that is exactly what he meant.

Trudeau the Justice minister had been in the vanguard in terms of personal mores. Had he not declared "The State has no business in the

---

1. Pierre Elliott Trudeau, *À contre-courant*. Textes choisis 1939-1996.

bedrooms of the nation" when he pushed his omnibus bill through the House in 1969? Yet, Trudeau the Prime Minister did not hesitate to send soldiers and policemen into the bedrooms of people whose ideas differed from his own. This paradox did not escape a man of the law like Thomas Berger: "What Trudeau had regarded as an outrage during the dark days of the Duplessis era had become, when he was prime minister in 1970, a state necessity." [2]

This article by *Gazette* reporter John Cruickshank tells the story of the nighttime arrest of Gaston Miron, poet. It was published on the tenth anniversary of the war measures under the title "Suddenly, the 4:30 a.m. knock on the door" (*The Gazette*, October 4, 1980).

When a well-known person is arrested in a dramatic manner, an entire community can find that its confidence and security are threatened. Ramsay Cook had understood this point. In his master's thesis in 1955—see an excerpt in Chapter 2—he recalled the case of Camillien Houde, the Mayor of Montreal who was arrested in August 1940 as he left City Hall, taken to an internment camp, and held for four years: "The case of Houde was surely a graphic example of what might have happened to many more French Canadians." Gaston Miron was a publisher, but above all he was one of the best-known poets in Quebec—when he died in December 1996, the Quebec government under Lucien Bouchard held a national funeral for him. Other artists and writers, Denise Boucher, Pauline Julien, Gaétan Dostie, Michel Garneau, Gérald Godin, Jean-Marie Da Sylva, were also arrested. Striking at them together "in the middle of the night" was like rounding up an entire community, and by no means the least important, since they were the artists, creators who bore the dreams and hopes of an independent Quebec, a fact that surely irked Mr. Trudeau the most

◆

Fourteen-month-old Emmanuelle Miron was the first to wake when four Quebec Police Force officers broke down the door of the family's St. Louis Square apartment.

It was 4:30 a.m., October 16, 1970. The War Measures Act had been in force for thirty minutes and the police were there to arrest Emmanuelle's father, Montreal poet and publisher Gaston Miron.

"Before I could get out of bed they were on me with their guns drawn," Miron said during an interview this week.

---

2. Thomas Berger, *Fragile Freedoms*, p. 209

"They shouted that I was under arrest and to be held incommunicado. They shut the bedroom door on my mother and daughter so that I couldn't speak to them."

Police rounded up about 250 Quebecers that night and another 215 during the following weeks. Some were held four to six months as suspected members of the FLQ.

Miron was dragged out of bed in his underwear and interrogated for three hours by QPF Sergeant Detective Laval O'Leary while the other officers searched his home.

"As I was questioned, I could hear my mother and my daughter crying in the bedroom," Miron recounted.

"My mother was staying with us because she was dangerously ill and had to go into hospital that morning."

Learning that the War Measures Act had been declared, Miron asked whether Canada had gone to war against the United States.

"They told me to shut up and that I no longer had any rights," the poet recounted. "They told me I had to ask permission to be able to speak."

As the police emptied salt and pepper shakers looking for explosives detonators, Miron's mind drifted to a conversation with an ardent Quebec federalist in Paris, 15 years before.

"This guy said I'd know when separatism came because there would be police at my door in the middle of the night breaking into my house without a warrant; throwing me in jail without a charge," Miron said.

"As the police took me off to prison, the thought struck me that perhaps we Quebecois were finally free."

The federalist in Paris was Pierre Elliott Trudeau, chief of the federal government cabinet that brought the War Measures Act into force.

One officer found a box of file cards with names, addresses and phone numbers in Miron's writing desk. "The police were convinced that they had found a list of FLQ members though it was only a catalogue of subscribers to my publishing house," the poet remembers.

"I told them to look under the letter 'P'. They were shocked to find Gerard Pelletier's name. Under 'T' they found P. E. Trudeau. It was all so crazy."

At 7:30 a.m. the poet was taken to Parthenais prison, where, Miron says, craziness turned to nightmare.

For the next twelve days, Miron would be known only as 11-CD-26, a detainee, suspected of supporting the Front de Liberation du Quebec

(FLQ). "We weren't held in prison—we were interned in a temporary concentration camp," he said.

"We weren't prisoners because prisoners have rights and duties. We had nothing, not even our names because they never used our names. They locked us up in solitary confinement, legally stripping us of our basic human qualities.

"Without rights you fall into 'No Man's Land.' Nothing may happen but anything can happen."

During the days of interrogation that followed, Miron discovered that both he and Gérald Godin were suspected of being the authors of the FLQ communiqués.

At the time Miron was vice-president of the Committee for the Protection of the Rights of Quebec's Political Prisoners. Robert Lemieux was the committee's lawyer and police regarded it as a possible FLQ front.

Miron was held in solitary confinement for eight days in a cell three of his paces wide and four paces long. He was not permitted to shower or to exercise until the ninth day when he was moved to a holding centre with twenty-six other detainees.

During interrogations he was struck by three facts: Police had a dossier on him that he deemed to stretch back almost ten years; they seemed to have information about private conversations; and the interrogators were more interested in information about the Parti Québécois than they were about the FLQ.

"The hardest thing was I didn't know what had happened to my daughter," he said.

"I knew my mother would have to go to hospital and I worried that Emmanuelle would be left alone. I worried too that she wouldn't know me when I got out."

Guards and interrogators had told Miron he could be held for as long as a year without being charged with a crime or given the right to an attorney.

"But it was an instructive period: I learned what liberty and power really meant, because I saw raw power in action," he said.

"One day I was a human being with rights and obligations. Within hours, I was a number with no rights being dehumanized. Doing that to a man is really exercising power."

When he was released, Miron found friends had taken Emmanuelle to safety in Hull. Three days after his arrest, neighbours noticed that

Miron's door at 269 St. Louis Square was standing open. They repaired the lock police had broken.

"Nobody would believe me then when I told them I had been imprisoned," he said.

"Nobody wanted to know."

Though his bitterness has dissipated, Miron is adamant that legislation should be drafted to prevent a recurrence of the October 1970 round-ups.

"Can you call a country democratic where a repetition of that situation is still possible?" he asks.

"I think not. Democracy must define each man's rights. It should defend each man's rights. But a democracy can never take those rights away if it is to remain a democracy."

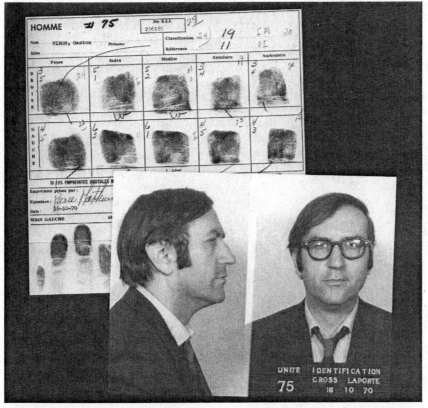

GASTON MIRON, poet and publisher, was arrested at 4:30 a.m. on October 16, 1970. When he died in 1996, the Quebec government organized a national funeral ceremony for him.

"I felt like a part of me had been destroyed."

Robert Fulford, alias Marshall Delaney

◆

EDITORS' NOTES

Massive arrests were key to the repression launched in the middle of the night on October 16, 1970. For each and every person arrested, it was a traumatic event. Very little has been written about that experience, especially in English. Quebec filmmaker Michel Brault, however, interviewed many detainees and made the fictional movie *Les ordres* in 1974, which won an award at Cannes and is now in the pantheon of Quebec cinema. Robert Fulford, editor of *Saturday Night*, was also a film critic who generally wrote under the alias of Marshall Delaney.[1] Fulford reviewed the film and all who have seen the film will agree that his observations brilliantly describe the Kafkaesque nature of the arrests made in October 1970. Fulford also goes one step further and links those arrests to universal truths. "Every society contains willing servants of totalitarianism: when the communists or the fascists take over there is never a shortage of guards."

To appreciate Fulford-Delaney's observations, it is important to grasp the scope of the arrests made in 1970. Here is how John Conway described them in *Debts to Pay.*[2]

◆

---

1. Robert Fulford explained how he came to use his own name in one publication and the nom de plume in another in his book *Marshall Delaney at the movies, the contemporary world as seen on film,* Toronto, P. Martin Associates, 1974. His review of *Les ordres* appeared in *Saturday Night* in 1975 under the title: "Canada's trauma produces a major work of art."

2. John Conway, *Debts to Pay, The Future of Federalism in Quebec,* (third edition) 2004, pp. 82-83.

As soon as the WMA was proclaimed, the arrests in Quebec began. Before the sun came up 242 people had been arrested (…) Those arrested, besides the core leadership of local PQ associations, included not only those suspected of FLQ sympathy, very broadly defined, but also labour leaders, community activists and organizers, separatists of all types, and those known for effective opposition to any of the three levels of government. By the end of the arrests some days later, 465 had been arrested, their homes and offices ransacked and searched, their families and neighbours terrorized. Of these, 403 were eventually freed without charge. Most were not even subjected to any kind of interrogation. Of the remaining 62, 32 were charged, but the government decided not to prosecute. At the end of the day, only 18 were convicted of minor offences, like complicity, or of being accessories after the fact (…). The people arrested were victims of state violence: often arrested in the dead of night; not allowed to inform family, friends, or employers about what had happened; held without charges or bail. Some lost jobs; others claim to have been verbally and/or physically abused by police and prison guards; all experienced terror, degradation, and humiliation. And that appears to have been the only reason most of them were arrested in the first place—a settling of political accounts and a warning of the possible costs associated with their political convictions and actions.

• • •

The marvellous thing about Michel Brault's film *Les ordres* is that it goes far beyond the War Measures Act, Québec, Canada, and 1970: it reaches a kind of universal dimension by forcibly readjusting the audience's views not only of the Montréal political prisoners it depicts but of all prisoners in all jails. We read every week in the paper that someone was picked up by the police, kept in jail for a few days, then released. We assume that this was a trifling incident, a mistake of no significant proportions. But of course most of us have no idea what it is to be in jail for even an hour, much less days. Brault tells us.

He shows us five characters: a textile worker and his wife, a social worker, a young man who is unemployed, and a radical doctor. Each has a fictional name, but each is based on one or more of the 450 innocent people who were picked up by the police after the War Measures Act was proclaimed. Their stories are composites, but the details are all drawn from Brault's sixty hours of tape-recorded interviews with fifty of the real-life victims.

For the time the film runs, the audience lives inside the experience of these people. Brault's direction is so involving, and his use of the actors so skilful, that our identification is complete. We watch them wakened in the night, we hear the screams of their children as the police pound on the doors, we are stuffed into the back seats of police cars, pushed, prodded, insulted, and humiliated. We identify with their degradation as they are stripped and examined, as their beards are cut off and their clothes taken away, as officious guards herd them like cattle.

Moreover, we grasp the extreme intellectual and spiritual deprivation a prisoner may suffer. A part of everyone's humanity is his connection with other humans and if you can control the information a prisoner receives, you can reduce him to a sub-human level. These people are cut off from two vital elements of humanity: their family and friends on the one hand, and the world of public events on the other. They don't know what's happened to their children or wives or husbands. No one can visit or phone them, and they can't phone out. The doctor's wife is about to give birth, so as the days in jail drag on he doesn't know whether he's become a father or not or whether she's in desperate trouble. Another man's father is dying and he knows nothing of it. Equally, the prisoners are shut off from the news; they don't know, for instance, that on the second day of their internment Pierre Laporte has been found dead; they have no idea of the hysteria now gripping the whole country, or of the chilling effects of the War Measures Act proclamation. They have thus ceased to exist as fathers, husbands, and citizens. The state has imposed on them a kind of temporary death.

The doctor, at one point, looks through the bars of his cell at another prisoner washing the floor. That man has a little more freedom than he does, and has something to do, so the doctor envies him. "Your whole life:" he says voice-over, "is turned upside down. All of a sudden it's a privilege to wash the floors. And you want that privilege!" Later, he looks back and says, "I think we'll all carry this scar the rest of our lives." The young unemployed man puts it even more clearly: "I felt like a part of me had been destroyed."

In his treatment of the policemen and guards, Brault provides the film with a kind of subtext. One of his themes is man's will to express his own grievances and resentments by humiliating, degrading, and ultimately destroying other men. The policemen and guards, his film suggests, are not doing all this just because (as one says). "We've got orders and we have to follow them." On the contrary, they are glad to do it; otherwise they couldn't perform with such passion and ingenuity. *Les ordres* makes in a fresh way the point that every society contains willing servants of totalitarianism: when the communists or the fascists take over there is never a shortage of guards because the things guards do are the things that come naturally to many men. The War Measures Act didn't create this negative force; it released it.

This is perhaps the most profound of the film's several messages. We need to have recalled to us that dictators and hoodlums are waiting among us, eager to take over. The only barrier that stands between us and them is the carefully and sensitively applied rule of law. The War Measures Act tore this barrier away. Most Canadians don't comprehend that yet, and perhaps *Les ordres* can help move us some slight distance toward understanding.

Michel Brault, who is now forty-six, has been one of the major figures of Québec cinema since its beginnings in the 1950s. He is almost certainly the finest cinematographer Canada has produced, and in France (where he has worked with the anthropologist filmmaker Jean Rouch) he has been classed among the world's best. He operated the camera for *Mon oncle Antoine* and *Kamouraska,* and those films demonstrate both his high craftsmanship and his versatility. In 1963 he was codirector with Pierre Perrault of *Pour la suite du monde* (*Moontrap*), the memorable feature-length documentary about some rural Québécois who revive their island's ancient skill of catching whales in the St. Lawrence. In 1967 he directed *Entre la mer et l'eau douce,* a beautiful though largely overlooked film that starred Geneviève Bujold and Claude Gauthier.

Brault uses [Claude] Gauthier again in *Les ordres,* this time as the unemployed young man whose jaunty dignity is stripped away by the guards. Gauthier gives a marvellously subtle performance, understating perfectly the slow destruction of the character. Jean Lapointe is the textile worker through whose eyes we see a large part of the film: he, too, handles highly dramatic material in a calm, clear, restrained manner. As his wife, Hélène Loiselle, seems to embody all the miseries of women who are placed on the receiving end of life's indignities. Toward the close of the film, when a petty official gives her back her freedom—freedom that should never have been taken away—she looks at him with pitiful gratitude. It's a moment to shame anyone who ever held power over another human being.

Brault's use of the material—he wrote the script and shared the camerawork as well as directing—is almost always on a high level. (Perhaps the one exception is his rather arbitrary use of colour film for some scenes, black and white for others.) Many of the scenes are so tactful and have such a feeling of artistic wholeness that they could be the work of, say, François Truffaut. *Les ordres* affirms Brault's permanent importance as a director and provides us with a major landmark in the history of Canadian cinema.

At the same time, it leaves questions unanswered. Part of its power, in fact, is the ability to make us want to know a great deal more about this crucial event in our history. Just as Brault omits all facts about public events of the moment (because his characters can't know them), so he ignores the specific guilt of the public officials involved. He never suggests why these 450 people were picked up rather than some other 450; who made the list? Nor does he inquire deeply into the background of his characters. He presumes their legal innocence in the FLQ activities, but he never touches on the more sensitive question of moral complicity. When we first meet these people, they are free and both James Cross and Pierre Laporte have been kidnapped. What do they think of those events? Are they delighted or appalled? Brault never hints at an answer, and for good reason: to know that might complicate, perhaps unnecessarily, our emotional involvement with their ordeal.

Les ordres is the first major work of art inspired by the trauma of October, 1970, but I hope it won't be the last. We still need to know a great deal more about what happened to Canada and its collective life in that period. The sad fact is that we forget much too easily. *Les ordres* brought this home to me with special vividness when the Lapointe character, in a rage, says to his guards: "Someday somebody is going to pay for all this." Wrong. Quite wrong. Nobody ever paid. They all got away with it.

6.2 In English Canada

"My students were frightened, concerned, and certain that Trudeau was the leader to put Quebec finally and firmly in its place."

Jack Granatstein

◆

EDITORS' NOTES

Several contributors were struck by the collective hysteria in Canada when the war measures operation was launched. A surprised Robert Fulford remarked, "The people were discovered to be hysterical. The press was shown as sycophantic." (See Chapter 7.) Parliamentary reporter Peter Reilly pointed out that the hysteria observed in Toronto was also present in Ottawa where decisions were made. Reilly was more struck by the public hostility towards Quebec as a whole than by the hate for the FLQ and violence. "The mood was hawkish on Quebec," he wrote in the December issue of *Saturday Night*. These feelings were cogently expressed in a quote from a Liberal Party member of Parliament. "The rednecks and the hard-hats voted for Trudeau because they thought he'd put down the frogs, and now it looks as though he's doing it. So they're behind it. I have the feeling he could order the troops to shoot every second person on sight and there'd be very little objection."[1]

Canada's capital and its politicians had no monopoly on hawkishness. It was also present in large cities like Toronto, and even on campuses, usually considered bastions of anti-government protest. Jack Granatstein was a young historian and professor of history in Toronto (where he was born in 1939). Professor Granatstein specializes in military history. He tells the story of a "Rally for Canada" during the war measures that involved more than five thousand students and faculty from York University to whom he and others were invited to speak. When Granatstein made very critical remarks about Trudeau and the war measures, he was met with anger from an aggressive crowd of students and academics. Thirty years later, he still had vivid memories of the "visceral hatred," the "vengeful mood," and the "anti-Quebec/pro-government response," but above all the

---

1. Ottawa Report, "The day the Uglies took over politics," *Saturday Night*, December 1970, p15.

extreme fear he felt as he spoke to what appeared to him to be a mob gone wild. "That day I was frightened," he wrote in the article below.[2]

From Jack Granatstein's story, it can be concluded that the fear provoked by the war measures was not only that which comes from seeing soldiers and policemen on the march, but also the fear that arises from contact with those—their numbers were far from negligible—who support and cheer on the soldiers, policemen, and their commanders.

Professor Granatstein wrote this text in 1998. Between 1970 and 1998, he had completely changed his mind and had come to support Trudeau. It is worth noting also that he had taken on new responsibilities. In 1998, when he wrote this article, he had been appointed head of the Canadian War Museum and he held that position until 2001. He also served his country in other ways. In 1994, he was part of the CBC's coverage of the fiftieth anniversary of D-Day. He helped Peter Mansbridge again on May 8, 1995 during the CBC's coverage of V-E Day. He reprised the same role on the sixtieth and sixty-fifth anniversary of D-Day and V-E Day. He is an Officer of the Order of Canada.[3]

◆

There had never before been a crowd at York University like it. Gathered around the flagpole in the centre of the still-growing campus that October noon in 1970 were at least five thousand students and faculty, pressed close together and surrounding the small stage. This was the university's "Rally for Canada," a response to the crisis in Quebec that had led the federal government to impose the War Measures Act and arrest almost five hundred suspected "terrorists" and their supporters.

The night before, one of my departmental colleagues, a young historian who had just arrived at York from Harvard University and who

---

2. "J.L. Granatstein, "Changing positions; Reflections on Pierre Trudeau and the October crisis," in *Trudeau's shadow: the Life and Legacy of Pierre Elliott Trudeau*, Edited by Andrew Cohen and J.L. Granatstein, Toronto, Random House of Canada 1998.

3. The 1998 text includes the following presentation of the author: "J.L. Granatstein is one of Canada's best-known academics, writers, and broadcast commentators. He taught history at York University from 1966 to 1995, and in 1998 became CEO and director of the Canadian war Museum. His many publications have focused on Canadian national history, Canada-US relations, the public service, universities, and the teaching of history. Although he never voted for Pierre Elliott Trudeau, he has supported Trudeau's constitutional views."

understood nothing whatsoever about what was happening, had called to ask me to speak at the rally. "But I don't support the government and its actions," I said. "That doesn't matter," came his very American reply, "come and speak for Canada."

So I did. There were other speakers, including historians Ramsay Cook and John Saywell, but in my memory I was the only one to oppose the government's actions forthrightly. I cannot remember my exact words, but I suggested that the imposition of the War Measures Act was a direct attack on the civil liberties of all Canadians, that it was using a mallet to kill a flea, and that, under its terms, not only the Front de libération du Québec terrorists but activists, hippies, Vietnam draft dodgers, and troublemakers could be arrested anywhere in Canada. That morning, the newspapers had reported that the mayor of Vancouver had greeted the imposition of the act with pleasure as a way to clean up his city.

I have never before or since been afraid of a crowd, never feared being torn limb from limb, but that day I was frightened. The shouts from the students that interrupted my speech were frequent and hostile; the visceral hatred of the FLQ kidnappers and murderers, and, as I interpreted it, of all Québécois, was palpable. I was very pleased to get off that platform and into my office before I was attacked and beaten.

The same vengeful mood pervaded my classroom the next day. One hundred students were enrolled in my third-year course on post-Confederation Canada, and I asked how many supported the government's policy. Every hand but one went up, a result that mirrored the national opinion polls. A Canadian Institute of Public Opinion poll taken on October 17 found that 88 percent of Canadians thought the government actions either not tough enough or about right; in Quebec, 86 percent felt that way. Understandably, none of the students was for terrorism, and everyone believed that Pierre Trudeau had acted with appropriate force to deal with the crisis created by the kidnapping of British trade commissioner James Cross and the kidnapping and murder of Pierre Laporte, Quebec's labour minister. Several female students referred to a comment by Jean Marchand, the minister of regional economic expansion who was also Trudeau's friend, that a woman had been found in Hull with "FLQ" scratched on her stomach. In other words, no one was safe. Marchand also painted the FLQ as having up to three thousand activists with weapons such as rifles and machine guns and two tons of explosives, and, for good measure, he labelled the Montreal civic action party, the Front d'action politique, or FRAP, which was fighting a city election against Mayor Jean Drapeau, as quasi-terrorists. Like the minister and the Quebec and federal governments, my students were frightened, concerned, and certain that Trudeau was the leader to put Quebec finally and firmly in its place.

It wasn't only students who felt that way. I recall very clearly a meeting of the board of the *Canadian Forum*, the left-centrist monthly of small circulation and, we fondly believed, much influence that had been publishing since 1920. Abe Rotstein of the University of Toronto was the editor, and we always met at his home. The question in the immediate aftermath of the FLQ crisis was what position the *Forum* editorial would take. The majority, of which I was part, was firmly for denouncing Trudeau's position, but a significant minority supported the government's actions. Ken McNaught, the University of Toronto historian and biographer of J.S. Woodsworth, was the main proponent of this view, and the discussion was fierce. In the end, the *Forum* attacked the government, and McNaught resigned from the editorial board. Years later, shortly before his death in 1997, he reminded me that at one point in the discussion I had threatened to punch him in the nose. Happily, I didn't.

Two years after the October Crisis, at a time when public opinion had begun to move massively against the Trudeau government and when many had begun to forget their strong anti-Quebec/pro-government responses at the time, the University of Toronto Press published *Forum: Canadian Life and Letters 1920-70: Selections from The Canadian Forum*. There was a grand party at Rotstein's house, and the book was hailed. At one point during the evening, Frank Scott, the constitutional expert, civil libertarian, poet, old socialist, and frequent *Forum* writer in the 1930s and 1940s, was asked to say a few words. In his celebratory remarks he referred to the *Forum*'s editorial about the imposition of the War Measures Act with a tone of mild criticism, and there were some kindly hisses—if hisses can ever be characterized that way, those ones were. I still remember the amazement with which I was soon hearing from people who hadn't attended the party that Scott had been shouted down because he still supported the imposition of the War Measures Act. Many professed pleasure that the socialist-turned reactionary Scott had been so treated. As that small incident suggested, the strong feelings about Trudeau's actions still persisted, though the swing in opinion was well under way.

Now, a quarter-century later, scarcely anyone appears to remember that the Canadian public, including the Quebec public, was solidly behind Trudeau and the War Measures Act in October 1970. A recent conversation with a young francophone journalist, to whom I told my story about the York rally, drew only puzzlement from her. You mean, she asked, that the students opposed you because you supported Trudeau? That it was the other way round she could scarcely believe.

"English Canada was not left unscathed by the hysteria and fear."

John Conway

◆

EDITORS' NOTES
John Conway is a sociologist and historian. He is professor of sociology at the University of Regina and served on the Regina Public School Board for many years.

He wrote an important book on Quebec and on the evolution of the historical relationship between Quebec and English Canada. The book is entitled *Debts to pay* and has come out in three editions, each with a different subtitle. This demonstrates the author's concern for ensuring the book remains up to date. The first edition in 1992 was subtitled, "English Canada and Quebec from the Conquest to the Referendum." In 1997, Conway chose the subtitle, "A Fresh Approach to the Quebec Question." Then in 2004, it bore the subtitle, "The Future of Federalism in Quebec." Conway devoted several pages of the book to the war measures.

Certain English Canadians, including Ontario Premier John Robarts,[1] were surprised to learn that the war measures applied to the entire country and not just Quebec. Yet how could measures invoked in the name of "national unity" be applied in any other way without creating an unfathomable contradiction? As a result, Quebec was not alone in experiencing the ordeal of war measures. The exact magnitude remains unknown since no full study has been conducted, but bits of information have been gathered. Some authors in this anthology provide examples. Hugh Segal, for instance, recalls in Chapter 8 a number of episodes that took place at his alma mater, the University of Ottawa, under the war measures. The University of Toronto student newspaper, *The Varsity*, reported the case of an American citizen living in Toronto who was arrested under the War Measures Act and threatened with extradition to the United States for charges unrelated to his conduct on Canadian soil.[2]

---

1. See text by Hugh Segal in Chapter 8.
2. "War Act is used to threaten man sought by U.S.," *The Varsity*, Friday, October 23, 1970.

In circumstances like those of October 1970, when fundamental free-doms are shunted away or totally eliminated, public opinion is usually "understanding" or even enthusiastic at first. A time comes, however, when people who had been cheering on government and police find themselves targeted by the repressive measures under way. This process as it evolved during the Second World War inspired the following comment in *The Globe and Mail* on October 12, 1940.[3] "It is the unpopular people who are the first victims of any Gestapo. The turn of the more reputable citizens comes next, when, having acquiesced in injustices being done to people they dislike, they find that their own shield against injustice has been destroyed." Once a repressive process gets under way, it becomes difficult to stop.

In this excerpt of *Debts to Pay*, third edition (2004), Conway shows how the war measures applied to Quebec soon made waves and caused damage thousands of kilometres away where they spread fear and hysteria and fostered the rise of censorship and unacceptable control measures by the police.

◆

English Canada was not left unscathed by the hysteria and fear. The B.C. cabinet passed an order-in-council requiring the instant dismissal of teachers or professors who, in the opinion of the police, advocated the policies of the FLQ. Seven members of the Vancouver Liberation Front, a student-based radical group, were arrested without charge and held over a weekend by Vancouver police. The mayor of Vancouver threatened to use WMA powers to clean his city of hippies and transi-ents. A student at Carleton University had his home searched in the first hour; nothing was found but he was taken to jail and held incom-municado for six days. A student at Ottawa University was arrested and held for four days because he happened to be called Bernard Lortie, the name of a known member of the FLQ. The editors of several university newspapers across Canada were visited by police and threatened because of their intention to print the FLQ manifesto. The Regina police chief expressed a desire to use the powers to clean out what he called "undesirable elements"—he had a notorious antipathy for hippies, stu-dent activists, indeed, for all young people with long hair. A Maple Creek, Saskatchewan, man, arrested for failing to produce a registration form and for having an unpaid 1967 parking ticket, was held in jail for

---

3. Quoted by Ramsay Cook in his Master's thesis. Signed J.V. McAree

three days. Former brigadier and then Regina Chamber of Commerce president Keehr advocated strengthening the militia by giving employees time off with pay for training so that Canada could better defend itself against a "bunch of kooks who think they can actually take over this country."

Then there was the extensive self-censorship by the media, often more vigorous than any government-appointed censor would have dared. Toronto's CHAN Television abruptly stopped a 60-minute taped interview show when it realized that the guest was a prominent Quebec labour leader who had been arrested in the first hours of the WMA. National CBC radio cancelled the broadcast of a Max Ferguson skit satirizing the WMA with a routine where Trudeau has been mistakenly arrested and held incommunicado. The CBC sent out a directive to all producers and directors ordering them to get on side with the government during the crisis. Government censors in Alberta banned the film *Red*, which featured a Métis who goes to Montreal. The airing of a TV documentary on Lenin, the Russian revolutionary leader, was cancelled. Mayor Drapeau told Quebec film censors to order the withdrawal of the film *Quiet Days in Clichy* from two Montreal theatres, or he would have the theatres raided and arrest everyone seeing the film, as well as the censors themselves. (The film was pulled.) Virtually every journalist and commentator active at the time in Quebec, as well as elsewhere in Canada, is full of stories of how censorship was imposed on his or her work during the crisis.

7

FRONTING THE STORM

7.1 In Parliament

"This is overkill on a gargantuan scale."[1]

Tommy Douglas

◆

EDITORS' NOTES

Parliamentarians had two opportunities in the fall of 1970 to speak out about the war measures, first, on Friday, October 16, just after the operation was launched, and second, in November during debate on the Public Order Act (Temporary Measures) tabled by John Turner on November 4. That Act is known as the Turner Bill. The first debate occurred during very dramatic moments on October 16 when everybody was talking about "apprehended insurrection." The debate was followed by the October 18 announcement that Pierre Laporte was dead. When the second debate took place, the political climate was somewhat calmer and people had begun to come to their senses.

Tommy Douglas, leader of the New Democratic Party, spoke out on October 16. He condemned the state terrorism, understood that the army had been called in, supported the government in its refusal to give in to the demands of the FLQ, announced that he was prepared to facilitate rapid adoption of new legislative measures, but categorically refused to go along with the fundamental actions taken by the Government of Canada. The reason was that the powers grabbed by the government effectively overturned the constitutional order of the country and threatened our most cherished rights and freedoms. "Right now there is no Constitution in this country, no Bill of Rights, no provincial constitutions. This government now has the power by Order in Council to do anything it wants—to intern any citizen, to deport any citizen, to arrest any person or to declare any organization subversive or illegal. These are tremendous powers".[2]

---

1. House of Commons, *Debates*, 16 October 1970.
2. House of Commons, *Debates*, 16 October 1970.

He also pointed out that the government had provided "not one shred of evidence" in support of its claims about apprehended insurrection. What had appeared obvious to him on October 16 had become a glaring fact by November. More specifically, the weaknesses of the government's arguments were so apparent that Tommy Douglas saw a pure demonstration of McCarthyism in action inspired by an overarching desire to put an end to political and social unrest, particularly in Montreal with the FRAP.[3]

Tommy Douglas was bitterly attacked for taking that position. In Parliament during a very rowdy session on October 16, he was heckled by shouts of "shame on you!" Public opinion was also hostile. He received about six thousand letters and ninety-five percent of them, according to his biographer, were hostile. Polls showed that his party lost a third of its support, which fell from twenty percent in October to thirteen percent in December.

Some people came to his defence nonetheless. In the heat of the action, Dave Barrett, a member of the British Columbia Legislative Assembly and future premier of that province beginning in 1972, declared: "Time will of course prove you right again."[4] Later, his biographer Donald Brittain, who was also a National Film Board filmmaker and who did a documentary on Douglas, said, "It was, perhaps, his finest hour. It was certainly his loneliest. But gradually the people came back to him, recognizing his courage and the rightness of his last great stand."[5] Doris Shackleton added that, "Douglas' single-handed opposition to the War Measures Act will be seen as the strongest single act of his career. Not to give in to a panic of that dimension takes a great deal of what is commonly described as guts."[6] The best tribute however came many years after he died from a political opponent and by no means a secondary one. Eric Kierans was a member of the government that Douglas had attacked so harshly in the House of Commons. "It was Tommy Douglas of the NDP who

---

3. The situation reminded him of wartime: "I want to remind you that in the 1940s the government of Canada passed regulations under the War Measures Act to intern all Canadian-born Japanese. I remember being booed off the platform in Vancouver for opposing that. People said: 'The government tells us there's a yellow peril, that these Japs are going to blow up railways and everything else.' What happened? We locked them up and confiscated their property. And at the end of the war Mr. King said, 'There is not a single proven case of sabotage by any Canadian-born Japanese'," in *Tommy Douglas, The Road to Jerusalem,* Thomas McLeod and Ian McLeod, Hurtig, Edmonton, 1987.

4. Doris French Shackleton, *Tommy Douglas,* Toronto, McClelland and Stewart 1975, p. 304.

5. *Touched by Tommy,* Edited by Ed and Pemrose Phelan, WP Whelan Publications. Regina 1990.

6. Shackleton, *op. cit.,* p. 299.

stood in the House, day after day, and hammered the government for suspending civil liberties (...) He showed political courage of the highest order."[7]

Douglas discussed Trudeau's position later: "Trudeau was possibly really hoodwinked into believing it was the beginning of a Quebec revolution by the separatists, the FLQ, and certain elements in the CNTU. I think he's very intelligent, it's hard to believe he could have bought this. The other explanation which may prove to be the right one is that he saw this as a chance to do two things—first, to crush the separatist movement (...) And, second, to convince English Canada that here was a strong man who could keep Quebec in its place."[8]

Tommy Douglas also discussed Quebec-Canada rivalry and Quebec's future. In 1971, he addressed New Democratic Party members during the leadership convention: "The danger of Canada disintegrating is very real. Nationalist sentiment is growing in Quebec and the jailing of FRAP candidates and Parti Québécois organizers last October had the effect of further escalating this polarization. This is a time of cool heads and national sanity."[9] The question remained important for Tommy Douglas as he told his biographer: "Separatism is not going to go away. The strong-arm methods aren't going to work. They never have. I don't want to see Quebec leave Confederation, but I wouldn't have one drop of blood shed to keep them in Confederation. It's possible we will have to work out methods to separate and then work out agreements, though I hope it won't come to that. It would be better than a civil war. The Americans are still suffering from the civil war they fought a hundred years ago."[10]

Members of Parliament voted in favour of the whole operation on Monday October 19. Tommy Douglas voted against the war measures and was backed by fifteen New Democratic members of Parliament, but four members of his caucus bolted and voted with the government, Frank Howard, Barry Mather, Mark Rose, and Max Saltsman. The motion was approved with 190 in favour and sixteen against. When the vote on the Turner Bill was taken, however, Douglas received the support of all the New Democratic members of Parliament and two Conservative members, David Macdonald (see his text below) and Roch La Salle, member for Joliette. The Social Credit members of Parliament also voted against the Bill, which meant that a total of thirty-one members voted against the government.

---

7. See Kierans in Chapter 4 of this book.
8. Shackleton, *op. cit.*, p. 298.
9. *Tommy Douglas speaks: till power is brought to pooling*, Edited by L.D. Lovick, Lantzville B.C., Oolichan Books 1979.
10. Shackleton, *op. cit.*, p. 305.

Thomas ("Tommy") Douglas was born in Scotland in 1904 and came to Canada with his family in 1919. He was ordained in 1930 and helped found the Co-operative Commonwealth Federation or the CCF in 1931, forerunner to the New Democratic Party. He was premier of Saskatchewan from 1944 until 1961. Tommy Douglas is known as the father of public health insurance in Canada. He became leader of the New Democratic Party when it was founded in 1961 and retired in 1971, to be succeeded by David Lewis. He died in 1986. In November 2004, Canadians voted Tommy Douglas "the Greatest Canadian of All Time" following a Canada-wide contest organized by the CBC. In the biographical notes prepared for the contest, the CBC wrote, "He took his final and most controversial stand during the October Crisis of 1970 when he voted against the implementation of the War Measures Act in Quebec. The move was devastating to his popularity at the time but he would be heralded years later for sticking by his principles of civil liberty." This echoes what Dave Barrett stated during the darkest hours of October 1970: "Time will of course prove you right again." Moreover, this book is dedicated to his memory.

His speech on the Turner Bill in Parliament on November 4, 1970 is the clearest expression of his opinions on the war measures.

◆

Mr. Speaker, the legislation now before us, to place on the statute books the Public Order (Temporary Measures) Act, 1970, represents another chapter in a series of events that began with the kidnapping of the British diplomat James Cross on October followed later by the kidnapping and obscene murder of Labour Minister Pierre Laporte.

At that time the members of the New Democratic Party in the House recognized the government's predicament. We gave it our support in refusing to accede to attempted blackmail by the FLQ, and we concurred in the federal government's decision to give to the provincial authorities all the help necessary to apprehend the guilty and to bring them to justice. Our quarrel with the government was when, in our opinion, they overreacted, panicked and invoked the War Measures Act, and enacted public order regulations for which the government asked the approval of the House on October 16.

In his opening speech today the Minister of Justice (Mr. Turner) appealed to the House to forget past events and to deal with this measure, and then he spent three-quarters of his time defending the government's decision to invoke the War Measures Act and attacking those of us who dared to vote against the government's motion presented to the House on October 16. I have no hesitation in saying that those of us who voted against that motion did so for two reasons: first, because we have not been given any evidence that there was a state of apprehended insurrection in this country and, second, because we could not approve the regulations enacted under the War Measures Act because they deprive Canadian citizens so extensively of basic civil liberties.

Let me deal briefly with those two questions. I said that we voted against the motion because we had no evidence that a state of apprehended insurrection obtained in this country. I want to say that now, more than two weeks since the War Measures Act was invoked, the government has not produced one shred of evidence, either publicly or privately, which would lead me to the conclusion that a state of apprehended insurrection existed in Canada on October 16. This is the kind of situation in which one cannot be dogmatic. It may be that when the government some day produces information which we do not now have, they may prove to be right; but as a Member of Parliament standing in my place I have no right to restrict the liberties of 21 million Canadians without adequate proof that a state of apprehended insurrection exists in this country.

When the government introduced this motion asking the House to approve the invocation of the War Measures Act, the Minister of Justice, the Minister of Regional Economic Expansion (Mr. Marchand) and the Minister of Labour (Mr. Mackasey) hinted darkly that the government possessed information which they could not give us at the time but which, when disclosed, would justify their action. Later, on October 21, I asked the Prime Minister (Mr. Trudeau) if we could have some of this information either publicly or, if it could not be given publicly at the moment, privately. The Prime Minister said the country has all the information there is. This, of course, seemed to contradict the statements of the Minister of Justice, and being an obedient servant the Minister of Justice told the House today that the country has all the information, that the House knows that there were kidnappings and a foul murder and that there was an anticipation of civil disorder. But that is not what the minister said to the House on October 16.

What he said appears at page 215 of *Hansard*. The Minister of Justice said: "It is my hope that some day the full details of the intelligence upon which the government acted can be made public, because until that day comes the people of Canada will not be able fully to appraise the course of action which has been taken by the government."

Where is this information which is some day going to be made known and which will fully justify and vindicate the government's action?

Government members are still struggling vainly to find some answers for the press who almost daily have been asking the government, "Where is the evidence of this apprehended insurrection?" The Minister of Regional Economic Expansion tried to help out. He went on a Vancouver radio program. He had told the House that there were between 1,000 and 3,000 supporters of the FLQ who had worked their way into vital posts in Quebec, and that the FLQ possesses thousands of machine guns, rifles, and bombs. Yet, Mr. Speaker, after nearly three weeks and having all the powers under the War Measures Act, so far as we know they have not found any cache of arms. They have arrested only 424 persons, of whom 359 have been released.

If the government knew there were these thousands of guns, bombs, and machine guns, if they knew there were 1,000 to 3,000 FLQ people in high posts, they must have known who they were and where they were. But what has happened? Was the minister simply drawing on his imagination? Are the forces of law enforcement in this country so incompetent that they have not been able to apprehend any of the people referred to by the Minister of Regional Economic Expansion?

Then the Minister of Regional Economic Expansion went one step further. In order to explain this unusual procedure of invoking the War Measures Act for the first time in Canada's history in peacetime, he said this was done to prevent bloodshed on the eve of the Montreal municipal elections, and he linked the FRAP municipal political organization with the FLQ. Not to be outdone, the mayor of Montreal next day described FRAP as being a haven for terrorists, criminals, and revolutionaries. Mr. Speaker, this is Canadian McCarthyism. This is guilt by association. All Canadians abhor the things which have been done by the FLQ, and so a minister of the Crown and the mayor of Canada's largest city immediately smear some political opponents by linking them in the public mind with the FLQ.

This is the worst kind of McCarthyism. The Minister of National Defence (Mr. Macdonald) had another alibi. He said that the reason for invoking the War Measures Act was that there were several stages to revolutions in other countries and that in Canada the final stage of a planned revolutionary timetable was about to begin. Revolution was about to break out in this country; the fourth and final stage was at hand. I ask, where are these revolutionaries? The combined police forces of Canada, of the province of Quebec and of the city of Montreal have been at work now for almost three weeks. Where are these revolutionaries? The Minister of Justice tells us today that out of 424 people who have been detained, 65 are still being held. If these 65 can start the revolution, they must be supermen or the government is trying to mislead the House and the people of this country.

Then, of course, in desperation the government found the final explanation for their unprecedented action, a plot for a coup d'état in Quebec. They said there was a plot to set up a provisional government in the province of Quebec. When I asked the Prime Minister about this, he said these were rumours started by the opposition and the press. But, Mr. Speaker, members of the press on television the night before last said they were told these stories by people very high up in the government. I asked if we could have an investigation to see who was telling the truth, but the Prime Minister did not seem to take kindly to that suggestion.

The Leader of the Opposition (Mr. Stanfield) has already quoted from the speech made in Toronto by the hon. member for St. Paul's (Mr. Wahn), a supporter of the government. He is not in the opposition; he is not in the press gallery. I will not quote all of it because the Leader of the Opposition already quoted it, but I quote the last paragraph of what the hon. member said: "As we now know, there was some evidence of a parallel government waiting in the wings, including members of elite groups such as the Estates General."

Surely the government has a responsibility to produce such evidence. There is a hint of treason here. If the government knows those in Quebec who were planning unconstitutionally and illegitimately to take over the government of Quebec, it has a duty and a responsibility to apprehend them, bring them before the courts and charge them with treason. But if the discussions were about the possibility of forming a coalition government to meet a crisis, surely this is within the purview of the members of the National Assembly of Quebec. Are we to take it that the federal government invoked the War Measures Act in order to make sure that only a Liberal government continued to rule in the province of Quebec? If so, that represents a major intervention in the political affairs of a province.

We have been trying for nearly three weeks to get the government to give us some evidence of the apprehended insurrection. We shall continue to try to get that evidence. I think the fact that the government has dropped any reference to a state of apprehended insurrection in this legislation is proof positive that it is not prepared to substantiate its contention of October 16. (...)

This government should either put up or shut up. On the question of apprehended insurrection the government apparently has decided to shut up. I suggest that the government has failed to demonstrate that kidnappers and terrorists could not be dealt with under the wide powers now contained in the Criminal Code. Perhaps the Minister of Regional Economic Expansion can explain why the government did not consider the criminal law adequate. On the program to which I referred a few moments ago he said: "It is not the individual action we are worried about now. It's this vast organization supported by bona fide organizations who are supporting, indirectly at least, the FLQ."

That is a serious statement, Mr. Speaker, and one which gives rise to many questions. Has the War Measures Act been used to settle political scores and to intimidate groups like the CNTU and the Quebec Federation of Labour? I think it is significant that to date most of those detained seem to be members of either FRAP or the Parti Québécois. Although I disagree with the separatists, it is not a crime to be one as long as they do not seek to use violence and unconstitutional means to advance their objectives.

The fact that the government felt it necessary to invoke the War Measures Act rather than come to Parliament and ask for any additional powers needed under the Criminal Code leads one to feel, from the statement made by the Minister of Regional Economic Expansion, that the motive is a much more serious one than we had appreciated on October 16. The second reason for our opposing the motion on October 16, Mr. Speaker, was that we considered the regulations enacted under the War Measures Act deprived Canadians of some of their most cherished, basic human rights. This afternoon the Minister of Justice said I had spoken frequently about the potential of the War Measures Act. Wherever I have discussed this matter I have spoken exclusively of the regulations which the government had passed under that act. In my opinion they are horrendous regulations, taking wide and sweeping powers.

As the persons who have been released get an opportunity to tell their story, I think it will become increasingly apparent that this wide net which the government spread under its regulations gathered in a great many more innocent people than guilty people. We in the New Democratic Party recognize the need for prompt and energetic steps to stamp out terrorism, but we have insisted from the beginning that in the process of stamping out terrorism we must not abridge the freedoms that our people and our forefathers have won for us over the years.

One of the things that concerned us when the government brought in these regulations was the fact that while the government drafted them, the administration of them would be in the hands of the provincial Attorneys General and local police officers. What has been the result? The result is that day after day the Minister of Justice stated in answer to questions that this matter is under the jurisdiction of the Attorney General of the province of Quebec. When we asked whether the detainees were being held incommunicado, whether their families will be notified, whether they will be given the right of counsel, he said that he would be glad to take up this matter with the Attorney General of the province of Quebec.

I say to the Minister of Justice, through you, Mr. Speaker, "You cannot wash your hands of this responsibility. You drafted these regulations and you must accept responsibility if they were so all-embracing that they allowed those administering them to violate basic freedoms of the Canadian people."

We need to know, and we are going to find out, how many persons were wrongfully arrested and detained. Will there be any compensation for those who have lost time from their employment? How many have lost their jobs as a result of being arrested? How many were held for days and then questioned for only a few minutes? How many were held incommunicado throughout the entire period of their detention?

The minister told us today that none of the sixty-five still detained have been charged. When we asked how many will be charged, the minister said he did not know because any charges will be laid by the Attorney General of the province of Quebec. This government has nothing to do with that. That is why it is such a serious matter for a government to pass regulations of a sweeping restrictive nature such as those now in effect, when the administration is in the hands of those over whom the government has absolutely no control. That is why the New Democratic Party opposed the sweeping powers contained in these regulations.

"Pierre Elliott Trudeau is the ideal solution
for English-speaking Canadians who want to settle
the Quebec problem once and for all."

David Macdonald

◆

EDITORS' NOTES
All observers of the war measures crisis, whatever their political stripe,
including some cabinet ministers, remarked on and often saluted the
courage exhibited by Tommy Douglas when he immediately denounced
the decision taken by the government in the middle of the night on
October 16. "It was his finest hour," said one.

The leader of the New Democratic Party was not the only member of
Parliament to demonstrate remarkable courage and clear-headedness.
David Macdonald, a Conservative, was another. Not surprisingly, his position has drawn less media attention, probably because he was still young,
but also because he was a backbencher from the smallest province and a
member of the Official Opposition that massively backed the leader's
position in favour of the war measures. Unlike Tommy Douglas, Macdonald
supported the government when the first vote was taken on October 19.
He quickly dug his heels in, however, and on November 4, 1970, in the
debate on the Turner Bill, he voted against sending the Bill to Committee
(he was the only member to do so). That was how he expressed his total
objection to the authoritarianism of the Bill, for which the government
bluntly refused to provide justification and which by then obviously had
no relationship with reality. David Macdonald was aware that things had
changed by November 4 and could not believe that the government
insisted on plowing ahead. In his final explanation of his own vote on the
Turner Bill on November 30, he hammered, "Why now, a month or six
weeks after the events of October 16? What new arrests…? What new
avenue of effectiveness…? Why until the end of April?"

Macdonald did not only speak out in the House of Commons.
Throughout those "doleful" months of 1970, as Ramsay Cook described
them, he continued to reflect on the question beyond the confines of

Parliament. This led him to express his profound concern at seeing what those events showed about the true nature of the Canadian political system. Three specific traits struck him: 1) the fragileness of our attachment to fundamental freedoms; 2) the very specific limits to our tolerance for dissent; and 3) the facility with which the government resorted to extreme measures, or what he called "the high degree of authoritarianism latent in Canadian society." This was the trait that appeared the most worrisome for the future of the country, particularly because it was at the heart of relations between English Canada and Quebec.

David Macdonald published that analysis in a short but very effective document entitled "Where the real danger lies" in the brochure *Strong and Free* (see below, 7.3). Reading that text helps understand why he concluded his remarks on the Turner Bill in the House on November 30 with, "One feels increasingly that the walls of misunderstanding have been thickened (…) and that now more than ever there are, in fact, two solitudes in this country."[1]

David Macdonald was born in Charlottetown in 1936. Ordained minister of the United Church in 1961, he was elected member of the House of Commons for Prince Edward Island in 1965, a seat he held until December 1979. He was Minister of Communications and Secretary of State in the Clark Government. In the 1988 general elections, David Macdonald was elected once again to the House of Commons, but this time to represent a Toronto riding. When the "Red Tory" Macdonald was defeated in 1993, he quit the Conservative Party and joined the New Democratic Party.

◆

The official explanation for the invoking of the War Measures Act and the subsequent temporary Public Order Bill must stand as a classic example of triple think and self-deception.

When the government announced the invoking of the War Measures Act its justification for such action was basically threefold: Firstly, it described a serious state of terror and possible insurrection in the Province of Quebec. Secondly, it indicated it was responding to requests from Quebec and Montreal governments. Thirdly, there was other information which, for obvious reasons, could not be disclosed at that time. Later, under increasing pressure to justify its intervention the official line was altered so as to enumerate the acts of violence and terror

---

1. House of Commons Debates, November 30, 1970, pp. 1612-1613.

.carried out in Quebec over the past half dozen years. Finally, when this was seen to be insufficient, a third explanation was forthcoming stating that because an insurrection had not occurred you could not prove that which had not taken place.

If the public's acceptance of this trilogy of explanation is astonishing, the gullibility of the Opposition parties is even more so. For not only did they accept the various interpretations offered at almost every step, but they gave the government the legitimacy which it so badly required. Not only did they accept the government's interpretation but they encouraged it to respond with appropriate legislation and, in particular, the temporary Public Order Bill (which: while milder in its repressive aspects than the War Measures Act and its regulations, was, in fact, more dangerous because of its statutory nature). The Opposition became a willing ally in the government's mythmaking by urging it to bring forth appropriate legislation to deal with the problem. Apart from mild objection and indecisive questioning as to what, in fact, the problem was, they happily concurred in government policy.

One of the amazing insights resulting from the invoking of the War Measures Act was the willingness of most Canadians to accept, without question, the suspension of many of their basic rights and protections under the law. It has been suggested that Canadians willingly allowed their civil liberties to be placed in cold storage because of the gravity of the situation. Yet, the logic of and the necessary relationship between these two events was never seriously examined. Canadians have traditionally regarded themselves as staunch defenders of human rights. The Canadian Bill of Rights passed in 1960 was proof positive, if such were necessary, that we hold strong belief in our basic freedoms. How important these rights are to us is a matter now in very serious question. Was our commitment to these various freedoms a commitment of the mind, heart and will? Or, was our commitment only similar to a religious or political tradition; important if exercised, of some use in identification if not. Either way, the commitment appears to have been of personal interest and little else.

A second virtue accepted as inherent to all Canadians was our tolerance for dissent. We have taken pride in a past which we believe to be most tolerant in accepting a divergence of opinions and ideals. Indeed, we have seen ourselves as more tolerant than most. When repressive waves of intolerance for political or religious ideals have swept other countries, we have kept our tolerance and remained cool. Indeed, we have taken comfort that such intolerance could not happen here. But those who now express public disagreement with the policy of the government regarding the War Measures Act, know not only that dissent is now unwelcome here, but is now regarded by many as dangerously close to subversion. In fact, when political figures have dared to disagree, they are met with charges of "playing politics" as if that alone was sufficient to indicate the selfish irresponsibility of the dissenter. As an aside, how anyone could imagine that political advantage could be gained from taking a position directly in opposition to that most widely supported, is difficult to understand. We have discovered in a time of perceived national crisis that we are no more tolerant of dissent than our neighbours to the south and in some respects a good deal less so. The Prime Minister well knew this when he indicated that he liked people to make clear choices and avoid "wishy-washy" thinking. He was pushing a polarization of public opinion which would make it easier, in his terms, to govern.

Perhaps the most disturbing element which has emerged from the crisis is the high degree of authoritarianism latent in Canadian society. For decades, this authoritarianism has been an accepted feature of Quebec political life, best evidenced in the concept and cult of "le chef". The Prime Minister in his earlier writings has specifically acknowledged this. Yet, what we have now learned is the even greater predisposition in English Canada for the imposition of "le chef". The primary acquiescence in October 1970 to "le chef" was not in French Canada, but primarily in English Canada. Trudeau said he knew what was best for Canada and Canadians accepted without question. The paternalism of his performance was gratefully received by a most willing English speaking Canada.

It would appear that the presence of Pierre Elliot Trudeau is, in effect, the ideal solution for English speaking Canadians who want to settle the Quebec problem once and for all. Beneath the veneer of polite acceptance and tolerance there has smoldered a resentment that feeds on long standing racial antipathy and misunderstanding coupled with more recent social and economic difficulties. It would have been impossible for English Canada to take a tough position with those who in their estimation have made intolerable demands on them if they had not found their ideal French Canadian. What was required was someone who had all the appearances of a French Canadian but who in reality saw the world in general and Canada in particular through Anglo Saxon glasses, as shaded as their own. They needed their "tame French Canadian." Posing, therefore, as a representative French Quebecer in Ottawa he has said and done all those things that they have longed to have happen. His response to delineated FLQ terror provided convenient cover in their view to "put them all in their place" and settle that "Quebec problem" for good. Quite obviously the dangers inherent in this outlook threaten the very existence of the country, and the freedom of every one of its citizens.

**"It is utter nonsense today
in the light of what we know."**

Grattan O'Leary

◆

EDITORS' NOTES

The Turner Bill was put to a vote in the Senate on December 2, 1970. Only one Senator opposed it. Grattan O'Leary was a Conservative Senator appointed in 1962. Though originally from Quebec, he was a Senator for Ontario where he had spent most of his professional life, first as parliamentary reporter and then editor of the Ottawa Journal.

When the war measures were imposed, O'Leary quickly understood what that meant for people's rights and freedoms: "This strikes at the very heart of all the freedom we enjoy." With the uproar following Pierre Laporte's death, however, the situation appeared to be so critical—"a crisis unparalleled since the 1837 Rebellion," he wrote in his memoirs—that he threw his support behind the government when the issue was put before the Senate on October 21.

His enthusiasm quickly waned when he saw that the FLQ was nowhere near as threatening as the government claimed. But most of all he did not understand why Prime Minster Trudeau refused to provide any further explanation when it was his duty to do so. "(The prime minister) is not sitting in the Kremlin; he is sitting in the Parliament of Canada and he is accountable. If you can invoke an act such as the War Measures Act (...), then surely the duty devolves upon you to tell the people why you had to do it."[1] He made the same point again a few years later in his Memoirs, which appeared shortly after he died in 1976: "What evidence did the government possess indicating a possibility of civil insurrection? None was ever forthcoming... Canadians are no wiser today as to the full ramifications of these dreadful episodes than they were then."[2]

---

1. Senate Debates, December 2, 1970, pp. 267-268.
2. Grattan O'Leary, *Recollections of People, Press and Politics*, Foreword by Robert Stanfield, Introduction by Norman Smith, Toronto, Macmillan of Canada 1977.

Michael Grattan O'Leary always considered himself to be a proud Irishman from Gaspé where he was born in 1888. "I am a child of Quebec. I was born within a few miles of the spot where Jacques Cartier planted his cross in Gaspé," he recalled in his Memoirs, and added, "I was and am a proud Quebecer." His ability to understand and identify with Quebec probably explain why in the whole October 1970 debate he was so disgusted by the contempt and scorn that he sensed in the public discourse regarding Quebec. "I was annoyed with those who said that this sort of thing happened only in Quebec. As one who boasts that two generations of those who began my days sleep in the soil of Quebec, I reject and resent that. I was reminded of Edmund Burke's statement, 'You cannot, sir, indict a people'."

◆

Honourable senators, I had no intention of speaking on this bill but I must say that having listened carefully to the words of my honourable leader (Hon. Mr. Flynn) this afternoon, and very carefully also to the words of the Government leader (Hon. Mr. Martin) last evening, I find it impossible to vote for this bill as it stands. I voted for proclamation of the War Measures Act, and like my leader I support the principle of this bill. But there are things in this bill which should not be in it, which need not be in it, and which I personally cannot support.

Every instinct of my being cries out against the fact that this bill provides for arrest without warrant. This to me is violation of an historic right, something that was won by men who stood on the high scaffolds and languished in dungeons; this strikes at the very heart of all the freedom we enjoy.

I listened a moment ago to my honourable friend Senator Hayden, for whom I have not only admiration but a great deal of affection, and he used words which, frankly, frightened me. It frightened me to think that someone of his intelligence, of his stature as a jurist, should use the words he did, in which he put liberty as a secondary thing in our lives. Liberty is not a secondary thing in our lives. Jefferson warned once that we should beware of frittering away liberty, which is precisely what is being done in this bill as it stands. All my honourable leader did this afternoon was to support the principle of the bill—and God knows, we all support the principle of this bill.

I was in the Province of Quebec last week. I talked to French-speaking people and English-speaking people and there is some fear and doubt about the means and methods and motivations of this

Government in proclaiming the War Measures Act and in bringing in this bill subsequently. We have had a series of contradictory, confusing and conflicting statements from the people who sponsor this legislation. We have one minister telling us that there are certain facts which can never be revealed. We have the Prime Minister of Canada telling us, "You have all the facts you need and all the facts you are going to get." You have one member of the Government telling us that there are 1,500 members of the FLQ in the Province of Quebec and the next day you have the Attorney General of the Province of Quebec saying this is nonsense, that there would not be more than 150 at most.

What does this bill mean? Does it mean that the Government still is apprehensive about an insurrection in Quebec? Have they said that? Do they still believe that the 150 members of the FLQ in the Province of Quebec are capable of an insurrection to overthrow the society and the Government in Canada? Surely this is nonsense. We all protested and we all were horrified about kidnapping and murder, but this bill is not based upon that. We are told it is based upon the continuing fear and apprehension of insurrection in the Province of Quebec. And the people of Canada today do not believe that nor do the people of Quebec believe it. The press of Canada does not believe it, and more and more there is growing doubt and dissatisfaction with the conduct of this Government throughout this whole situation.

Of course, the Government had to use the War Measures Act in the beginning. I hear and I read about the heroic action of the Government in doing this, which again is nonsense. It would only have been heroic had they not done it, because there was overwhelming support for something like the War Measures Act when Mr. Laporte was murdered and Mr. Cross was kidnapped. These are things different from apprehended insurrection now. Does the Government really mean that at the end of April the FLQ will have gone away? This is nonsense. What do they do if it has not gone away? Will they still have, which I do not believe they have, an apprehension of insurrection?

The Government, in my view, and I admit I am a prejudiced observer, overdramatized this whole thing. I am afraid there were those who tried to play politics with this thing and—got great credit for some heroic action they took when they took no heroic action at all. They only took the action any government would have taken and been compelled to take, and that is all. Why continue this? Why continue these contradictory statements? Why do we have the Minister of Justice telling us there are facts which perhaps may never be revealed? Why does the Prime Minister the next day repudiate him and say, "You have all the facts"? It seems to me the people of Canada at this time are entitled to know more facts than they have been given and that they are entitled to have a clearer explanation from the authorities of why this bill has been brought in, that they are entitled to know why people can be arrested without a warrant, even now, when it is quite clear that the FLQ never had the organization, never had the brains, never had the wealth or the connections to bring about an insurrection.

It is utter nonsense today in the light of what we know to suggest that a few murderers, a few fanatics in the Province of Quebec, who are disorganized, unorganized and mentally incapable, as their evidence has shown, would bring about an insurrection threatening Government and society in Canada.

I believe in the principle of this bill, because it is at least an improvement on the other, but still as it stands there are things in it which I cannot condone, which my conscience does not permit me to support. With all my history and my beliefs since I was a boy, I could never stand in this house and vote for an abridgement of liberty such as this, and condemn a man for doing something when it was legal and tell him that we have made it a crime later on. This is what the bill does.

I have heard all your legal arguments. There is no question about it that a man can be apprehended and can be brought into the court without a warrant and made to explain why he went to a meeting of the FLQ six months ago. The first time I saw my distinguished friend was at a Conservative convention. Would he want to be tried and convicted because of that now? What retroactive legislation? This retroactive legislation is impossible in a civilized society, and yet my great friend and distinguished jurist has said, in effect, that the liberty of the subject is not as important as some other things, that the liberty of the subject is not the most important thing in our lives. No law, no legal sophistry, no legal quibbles can support that. That to me is basic and fundamental and this house will deserve and invite disrespect if it is not prepared to stand up now and make sure that this bill, that this proposed law, does not invade the liberty of the subject. Law, yes, but law sustained by liberty. That is what Macaulay said, "law sustained by liberty and liberty sustained by law" but he put liberty first and so do I. And that is why, unless this bill is amended, I certainly shall vote against it.

7.2 In the Media

**"The people of Canada believe, not in civil rights,
but in civil rights when they are convenient."**

Robert Fulford

◆

EDITORS' NOTES

Support for the war measures was massive in Parliament. Polls indicated equally massive support among the general population, topping eighty-five percent. In everyday life, opposing the war measures was a sure way to compromise one's reputation as a good patriotic citizen, as parliamentary dissident David Macdonald deplored in his speech quoted above. "Those who now express public disagreement re the War Measures Act, know not only that dissent is now unwelcome here, but is now regarded by many as dangerously close to subversion." People who opposed the war measures also ran the risk of losing their jobs. On October 16, 1970, morning man Rod Dewar at Montreal's CJAD radio station was immediately suspended after he dared to say, "I went to bed in a democracy and awoke to find myself in a police state."[1]

This state of public opinion was also reflected in the media who, as Thomas Berger wrote, "constituted themselves a cheering section for Trudeau and his government".[2] People spoke up nonetheless. James Eayrs

---

1. "Commentator quit CJAD over War Measures Act," *The Gazette*, March 10, 2010.; "Told he was suspended for a week, Dewar rushed into the studio and quit on-air.
2. Thomas Berger, *op. cit.*, p. 211. For the backdrop of "fear, panic, and hysteria," see Conway's description in *Debts to Pay*, pp 84-85: "Fear, panic, and hysteria became general, affecting the whole country, touching down here and there with sometimes comic, other times malevolent, results. Much of this mood resulted from a deliberately orchestrated campaign by the governments involved to justify their actions. The really serious fear campaign began with the imposition of the WMA and intensified with Laporte's death. Claims were made that the FLQ had infiltrated all key institutions of Quebec, that three thousand armed FLQ terrorists were ready to begin an insurrection, that the FLQ had a "hit list" of two hundred Quebec leaders marked for assassination, that the kidnappings were just the first step in a revolutionary plan—next, there would be mass meetings, then a massive bombing campaign, then a bloodbath of executions, all followed by the installation of a provisional government. No scenario was too fantastic, no tactic too bizarre, to be blurted out by one prominent politician or another. The media, which had been somewhat balanced though sensationalist before the imposition of the WMA, got clearly on the government's side after the proclamation, reporting as fact every wild exaggeration and every fantastic notion."

did so in his columns in *The Toronto Star*, others did so strongly in the *Canadian Forum*. Robert Fulford, editor at *Saturday Night* also strongly expressed his opposition to the war measures.

In the December 1970 issue of *Saturday Night*, Robert Fulford indignantly and virulently attacked the government—"totalitarian in spirit"—and its ministers who were too cowardly to protest. He denounced the ineffectiveness of the opposition parties, reproached the provinces for their complete absence. As regards the media, which was his world, he called it nothing less than "sycophantic." However, the most shameful aspect was that the citizens were completely behind the government: "The people of Canada *wanted* their fellow citizens' rights denied," an analysis that is shared by others in this book, including Robert Stanfield in Chapter 8, "Hindsight."

Fulford also wondered, "whether such monstrous regulations are justified *even in actual wartime*" (Fulford's italics), and then asked the rhetorical question, "Does democracy best defend itself by destroying democracy?" This principled position, which ran strongly against the current, unwittingly echoed another question raised twenty-two years earlier. In 1948, a Canadian intellectual by the name of Pierre Elliott Trudeau, then a student in London wrote, "[in time of war] the citizen has the overriding obligation to keep an even closer watch on his government than at any other time; to criticize without pity those whose increased prestige and work could lead to choose authoritarian solutions. The citizen must rise up in opposition to the idea that a tyrannical law must be condemned in time of peace, but applauded in time of war." [3]

This is the article Robert Fulford published in December 1970 under the sober, eloquent, and courageous title "Against the War Measures Act."

◆

In the great October crisis of 1970, Canadian democracy was tested and found wanting. The Trudeau Government was revealed as totalitarian in spirit. The people were discovered to be hysterical. The press was shown as sycophantic. The provincial premiers and the official Opposition in parliament turned out to be, in a crisis, useless. Looking back from just this distance, it already seems a profoundly shameful moment in our history. Professional historians, writing with more detachment twenty or thirty years from now, may rate it even worse than that: they may see it as a time when the basic freedoms of Canadian life began an inexorable process of erosion.

In Montreal that first terrible week of the War Measures Act, hundreds of Canadians were arbitrarily denied their rights—their right to

---

3. See Trudeau's "letter from London" in Chapter 2 above.

liberty, their right to counsel, their right to know why they were being held in jail, their right to communicate with relatives and friends. They were stripped, by an order of the federal cabinet, of all the personal rights that hundreds of years of history had bestowed on them.

The worst of it all was the lack of effective protest. On Friday, October 16, the morning when the War Measures Act was proclaimed, the most significant fact was that not one member of the federal cabinet resigned. The government's action was clearly arbitrary in the worst sense: surely, I reasoned, reading the papers that day, at least *one* of those twenty-nine men had the soul of a civil libertarian? But no. Not one. They all just sat there and took it.

In the days that followed, the reason was clear. Those silent men in the cabinet, and the many MPs who later sat silent with them, had correctly judged the public mood. The people of Canada *wanted* their fellow citizens' rights denied; they wanted those (alleged, supposed, possible) FLQ sympathizers thrown in jail. Thus the Canadians revealed that their most cherished beliefs were basically fraudulent.

The people of Canada, it turns out, believe not in civil rights but in civil rights when they are convenient; we believe not in individual liberty but in individual liberty when it does not get in the way of orderly government. Above all, we believe essentially in liberty for us, not for *them*.

To anyone but an hysteric it was obvious from the beginning that the federal government was dead wrong. Without invoking the War Measures Act, Ottawa had all the laws necessary to seek out the kidnappers and murderers and plotters. It had all the laws necessary to keep the army in place as support for the police.

The government pleaded, through the hints of various ministers, that there was something truly unthinkably awful going on; that the War Measures Act, with its many fascist-type provisions, was a necessity. The government couldn't tell us exactly *what* was going on, but if we would just trust the government for a while then…

To their lasting shame, most Canadians—including most of those who call themselves civil libertarians—decided to trust the government and abandon their liberties. But in fact there was *nothing* the government could say that would have justified such an action—not bombings, not more kidnappings or murders, not hijackings, not even an armed insurrection. Indeed, anyone who cares about liberty, and who reads the War Measures Act and the regulations the government promulgated under it, will wonder whether such monstrous regulations are justified *even in actual wartime*. Does democracy best defend itself by destroying democracy?

If the government was wrong, why did it do what it did? I'm not sure we'll ever know: certainly the question will be argued on half a dozen levels, for many years.

One answer is that this is, above all, a *neat* government. It likes to handle things in the most convenient way. And the War Measures Act, which gives the government the right to do exactly anything it wants, is the most convenient statute ever passed by a Canadian parliament. It replaces cluttered, messy, slow-moving British justice with the clean, hard-edged efficiency of totalitarianism. In times of crisis, the War Measures Act is the neat man's natural resort.

But there may have been another, more clearly political reason. The War Measures Act was—so it must have seemed in Ottawa—a way to delegitimatize extremist feeling in Quebec, to throw an aura of crim-inality over all dissent to the left, say, of the Parti Québécois (and maybe to parts of the PQ itself). In this sense the War Measures Act might have been expected to solve one of the country's major political questions: in this sense the FLQ kidnappings provided, for the government, an excuse.

Of course, for most elements in the government this would have to be (one hopes) a subconscious desire. But it would he no less real for that.

7.3 In Public Opinion

**"The freedoms of all Canadians are too sacred
to be threatened by either a group of political criminals,
or an arrogant government."**

STRONG and FREE[1]

◆

EDITORS' NOTES
Hugh Segal and David Macdonald strongly opposed what the Trudeau government was doing. Segal was a history student at the University of Ottawa and president of the Students' Federation. Macdonald was an Anglican minister and member of Parliament for Prince Edward Island in the House of Commons.

They both publicly denounced the war measures and made a point of convincing others to do the same. They obtained support and published a pamphlet in late fall 1970 protesting the war measures that bore a title that echoed the country's national anthem, O Canada. *Strong and Free... Nos foyers et nos droits.* Following are excerpts from the introduction.

◆

" *Strong and free...* is not a diatribe. It is not a political manifesto. It is a statement by some worried Canadians (...)

"The War Measures Act and the Public Order Act have changed the history and future of this country very directly. The contributors to this pamphlet feel that the introduction of both acts was not only unnecessary, but representative of the worst type of political arrogance and authoritarianism that any government can be found guilty of. Those who refused to shoulder the responsibility of opposing these acts, must share in that guilt. (...)

"The freedoms of all Canadians are too sacred to be threatened by either a group of political criminals, or an arrogant government. And by the very means by which the government chose to invoke the name

---

1. *Strong and Free, A Response to the War Measures Act*, Toronto/Chicago, New Press 1970.

of freedom, they eroded irreparably that very freedom which they were thriving to uphold. (…)

"A civilized nation, with sane government and a system of law, need not lower itself to declaring war on a group of criminals.

"A civilized nation should look less at the symptoms and more at the causes of terror and disaffection.

"The contributors believe Canada to be such a civilized nation. And that is why we must all join together in bringing her back to democracy."

◆

EDITORS' NOTES
The list of eleven contributors read as follows: George Bain, associate editor and Ottawa columnist of the *Globe and Mail*. Alan Clarke, formerly director of the Canadian Citizenship Council and the Company of Young Canadians, and then director of the Demonstration Project in Community Development at Algonquin College. Dian Cohen, Montreal economist, writing with *The Toronto Star*. Peter Desbarats, associate editor of *Saturday Night*, and a host of CBC-TV's *Hourglass*. James Eayrs, professor of international relations at the University of Toronto. James Littleton, consultant with the National Film Board and a writer. David Macdonald, Member of Parliament for Egmont, Prince Edward Island. Nate Nurgitz, Winnipeg lawyer, national president of the Progressive Conservative Party. Claude Parisée, président du Parti Québécois, comté de Hull. Hugh Segal, a Montrealer studying at the University of Ottawa, and president of the Students' Federation. Pat Watson, independent broadcaster and producer.

This pamphlet was published during the most intense period of the war measures crisis and it was also signed by some fifty personalities from all walks of life. The list of names appeared under the following note: "This book expresses a variety of thoughts which the following Canadians felt should receive wider circulation to stimulate further public discussion."

◆

ONTARIO:
Norman Atkins, Toronto
Henry Best, Toronto
Claude Bissell, Toronto
June Callwood, Toronto

Dalton Camp, Toronto
A. P. Cohen, Kingston
Ramsay Cook, Toronto
E.A. Goodman, Toronto
George Grant, Hamilton

Roger Graham, Kingston
Alan C. Holman, Ottawa
Tom Hockin, Toronto
Pauline Jewett, Ottawa
William Kilbourn, Toronto
Jim Laxer, Kingston
William Macadam,Ottawa
Flora MacDonald, Kingston
Robert B. McClure, Toronto
Roy McMurtry, Toronto
John Meisel, Kingston
George Perlin, Kingston
Abraham Rotstein, Toronto
H. R. S. Ryan, Kingston
William Saywell, Toronto
Donald Smiley, Toronto
Denis Smith, Peterborough
Melville Watkins, Toronto

WESTERN CANADA:
Lloyd Axworthy, Winnipeg
Tom Berger, Vancouver
John Courtney, Saskatoon
Waldren Fox-Decent, Winnipeg
Charles Gordon, Brandon
Charles Huband, Winnipeg
Jack Johnson, Calgary
David W. Kilgour, Winnipeg
Ruth Krindle, Winnipeg
James A. Macaulay, Vancouver
Mel Myers, Winnipeg
Nate Nurgitz, Winnipeg
Harry Rankin, Vancouver
R.A.H. Robson, Vancouver

Doug Rowland, M.P., Selkirk
John Stanton, Vancouver
Hon. H. H. Stevens, Vancouver
Max Wolfe, Calgary
Gordon Wright, Edmonton

MARITIMES:
Donald Cameron, Fredericton
John Carter, St. John's
Muriel Duckworth, Halifax
Gordon Fairweather, M.P.,
Fundy-Royal
Nick Fillmore, Halifax
Brian Flemming, Halifax
Lionel Guravich, Saint John
Keith Jobson, Halifax
Brenda Large, Halifax
Marilyn MacDonald, Halifax
Carol Ann and David Nicholson,
Fredericton
Lloyd Shaw, Halifax
Denis Stairs, Halifax

QUÉBEC:
Guy Beaugrand-Champagne,
Outremont
Leo Dorais, Montreal
Claude Gousse, Montreal
Hubert Guindon, Montreal
Delmas Levesque, Montreal
Michael Oliver, Montreal
Marcel Pepin, Montreal
Claude Ryan, Montreal

**"The War Measures Act is being used (…)
as a means to silence political opposition."**

C.B. Macpherson, Dick Beddoes, Barbara Frum, et al.

◆

EDITORS' NOTES
The University of Toronto student newspaper, *The Varsity*, published a declaration signed by twenty eminent Canadians on March 3, 1971.[1] Signatories included many high-profile journalists, academics, musicians and political personalities. *The Varsity* specified that all three major Toronto dailies refused to publish this declaration and the names of those who signed it. For the record:

◆

"The federal government, contrary to its implied promises of last October, produced no evidence to justify the use of the War Measures Act and the passage of the Public Order Act.

"These Acts are being used not to prosecute criminal activity but to suppress political opinion in the same way opinion is suppressed in fascist and communist states. Since these are federal Acts, all Canadians must accept responsibility for this situation.

"The trials of those charged under the WMA are not criminal but political trials. Canadians now face prison sentences not for what they do but for what they think and say. We do not refer to the charges relating to kidnapping and murder.

"The War Measures Act is being used, therefore, not as most Canadians expected it to be used—to oppose violent revolution—but as a means to silence political opposition.

---

1. "Profs petition against War Measures Act," *The Varsity*, March 3, 1971.

"We believe freedom and democracy in Canada will be best served if the federal government withdraws the Public Order Act immediately, and if the Quebec government withdraws the indictments under the War Measures Act. We urge that the Canadian and Quebec governments be petitioned to do so.

"Last, we urge especially that English-speaking Canadians, who have been shamefully silent on this issue, speak out against the perversion of Canadian justice.

Dick Beddoes, journalist
Hans Blumenfeld, town planner
Stanley Burke, TV journalist
Reverend James Fisk
Barbara Frum, TV journalist
Dr. Northrop Frye, professor
Robert Fulford, journalist
Bruce Kidd, teacher
Anton Kuerti, pianist
Dr. James Lorimer, economist
Dorothy Mikos, journalist
Nancy Meek, artist

John Pocock, artist
Abraham Rotstein, economist
Clayton Ruby, lawyer
John Sewell, alderman
Geraldine Sherman, broadcaster
Grant Sinclair, law professor
Barnie Stuart, law professor
Melville Watkins, economist
Avrom Isaacs, art dealer
C.B. McPherson, political scientist
Kathleen McPherson"

7.4 Among Writers

"Why talk when you are helmeted with numbers."
Margaret Atwood

◆

EDITORS' NOTES
Margaret Atwood was in England when she learned what was happening in Canada. In protest and in solidarity, she formally joined Amnesty International in London. During the following months, she wrote the untitled poem published in the March 1971 issue of *Saturday Night*. The title is "Untitled", as though the absence of words best describes the silence that was imposed by the powers that be, "Why talk when you are helmeted with numbers."

Almost forty years later on April 19, 2009, on Radio-Canada's Sunday night flagship talk show, *Tout le monde en parle*, she responded to host Guy-A. Lepage's question about October 1970. Lepage recalled that in 1980 Margaret Atwood had already said, "If you think that Canada is really a democratic country where the freedom of expression reigns, you must remember the War Measures Act." Margaret Atwood then said in English on the French-language television, "I was in England at the time (…) It was quite horrifying to me that people were being arrested without proper warrant and put in jail and held there for indefinite length of time. So our democratic rights rest on very thin ice all the time." After a pause she added, "Every time there is a crisis, people want to take those away because it gives them more power. So we always have to be very attentive to those situations."

◆

Untitled

We hear nothing these days
from the ones in power

Why talk when you are a shoulder
or a vault

Fists have many forms;
a fist knows what it can do

without the nuisance of speaking:
it grabs and smashes.
From those inside or under
words gush like toothpaste.

Language, the fist
proclaims by squeezing
is for the weak only.[1]

---

1. Margaret Atwood, "Untitled," *Saturday Night*, March 1971, p. 8.

> "The leaders in the opposition raise questions. The leaders
> of the government raise guns against the people."
>
> Mervyn Procope

◆

EDITORS' NOTES
Artists and writers have played a leading role in the Quebec independence
movement since the 1960s. People in Quebec cultural circles, including
some of Quebec's best-known artists, were among the first to be targeted
in the war measures round up. Gaston Miron's story is recounted in Chapter
6. Historian Desmond Morton maintains that that was one of Trudeau's
main aims when he invoked the war measures.

   A number of English Canadian artists and writers spoke up against the
war measures during the October Crisis. The *Canadian Forum* ran poems
by people such as James Baque, Eli Mandel, Al Purdy and more. It also
published this poem by Mervyn Procope entitled "October 1970: War
Measures"

◆

October 1970: War Measures

The leaders in the opposition
Raise questions.
The leaders of the government
Raise guns against the people.
   I had a dream
   I talked with Mr. True North
   Strong and free.
   I told him I heard him saying
   All the old things governments say
   When they need to protect their nakedness.

    I told him,
    We have had enough plastic fig leaves
    In this cold country,
    Why should we create another tyranny.
    I told him,
    I believe that I know this country.
    This country seeps into me
    As water into Lake Superior.
    I woke up and found myself
    In the Quebec Provincial jail.
Indian Summer,
Frost rests on the stone,
Leaves fall to keep earth warm.
Liberty, a skinny calf,
Hangs in cold storage.[1]

---

1. Mervyn Procope, "October 1970: War Measures," *Canadian Forum*, March 1974, p. 14.

8

IN HINDSIGHT

"What is most significant and revealing
is that the public enthusiastically approved,
and since then never wanted any account."

Robert Stanfield

◆

EDITORS' NOTES
Robert Stanfield (1914-2003) was premier of Nova Scotia before being elected leader of the federal Conservative Party in 1967. During the war measures crisis, he was Leader of the Official Opposition in the House of Commons.

On that infamous Friday, October 16, he found himself torn between his instinct as a Red Tory and a gentleman on the one hand, fully aware of the threats to democracy in Canada that the proposed government law represented, and the politician's instinct about the state of public opinion on the other. His biographer pointed out that "he either had to endorse what clearly was an unprecedented peacetime violation of civil rights or expose himself and his party to the fury of an enraged public enthusiastically rallying to support what it chose to regard as the decisive leadership of Trudeau."[1]

He chose to back the government in the October 19 vote. (His entire caucus went along with him.) He expressed some reservations in the first debate in the morning of October 16, but obviously to no effect. As his other biographer Geoffrey Stevens wrote, "It made him seem dreadfully wishy-washy."[2]

Public opinion must have been powerful, since six weeks later he also agreed to vote in favour of the Turner Bill (as did all his members of Parliament with the notable exception of David Macdonald and Roch La Salle). Moreover, he surely understood that the situation was nowhere near as dramatic as the government had claimed.

---

1. Richard Clippingdale, *Robert Stanfield's Canada, Perspectives of the Best Prime Minister We Never Had*, McGill/Queen's 2008.
2. Geoffrey Stevens, *Stanfield*, Toronto, McClelland & Stewart 1973.

It is never too late to set the historical record straight. Although Robert Stanfield lacked courage in 1970, time did its work. After stepping down as leader in 1976, he revisited the 1970 crisis and said exactly what he thought on two occasions.

In January 1979, Ron Haggart and Aubrey Golden invited him to preface the second edition of their book entitled *Rumours of war*.[3] Then in 1980, the Canada West Foundation invited him to address its members on the theme *The Kind of Canada I Want*. The text of the preface is available and passages are provided below. The remarks he made before the Canada West Foundation are not available, but his biographer Clippingdale included the notes he used on that occasion.

He expressed disagreement with the action taken by Trudeau and deplored that despite government promises and the passage of time "no serious attempt was made at the time or has since been made to support the claim of an apprehended insurrection." He noted that throughout the war measures crisis, Trudeau "never said flatly that there was an apprehended insurrection." Stanfield, however, was most disappointed by what appeared to him to be Canadians' tenuous attachment to civil liberties. In his notes he even spoke of his "numbing disillusionment" which "gave me a much poorer opinion of my own countrymen re: civil liberty," adding that, "Canadians will accept improper means of achieving goals they desire" (Clippingdale, p.17). In making that harsh observation, Stanfield shares the opinions of others, such as Robert Fulford in December 1970 or Hugh Segal in 1996. All three echo the observation made by the young historian Ramsay Cook in his 1955 master's thesis on "Canadian Liberalism in wartime," also included in this anthology. In 1970, things had not changed since the Second World War. It is therefore up to democratically minded people to ensure they have changed since 1970. Following is a large section of Robert Stanfield's 1979 preface to *Rumours of war*.

◆

The invocation of the War Measures Act in October 1970 was surely one of the more significant and most revealing events in the history of our country. It was dramatic, it was ruthless, it was based on assertions which have never been factually supported, it involved injustice to hundreds of Canadians; but it was and presumably still is approved

---

3. *Rumours of war*, Ron Haggart and Aubrey E. Golden; with a new introduction by Robert Stanfield, James Lorimer & Company, Publishers, Toronto 1979. First published by New Press Toronto 1971.

by an overwhelming majority of Canadians, and we think of ourselves as a freedom-loving people.

The invocation of the War Measures Act enabled the federal government to authorize the police to arrest without warrant, and to detain without laying any charge and without bail—basic departures from our traditions of justice. The simultaneous use of the armed forces to reinforce civilian police in Québec was quite a different matter—it did not require the War Measures Act and in itself involved no breach of traditional rights.

The War Measures Act was invoked on the grounds of an apprehended insurrection in Québec and its application was limited to Québec. No serious attempt was made at the time or has since been made by the federal government to support the claim of an apprehended insurrection. In justifying his decision, the Prime Minister relied heavily upon letters from the governments of the province of Québec and the city of Montréal requesting emergency powers. "According to information we have and which is available to you," wrote the premier of Québec to Mr. Trudeau, "we are facing a concerted effort to intimidate and overthrow the government and the democratic institutions of this province through planned and systematic illegal action, including insurrection." However, neither the premier of Québec nor the mayor of Montréal presented any facts to justify such an assertion of planned insurrection.

Two prominent public men had been kidnapped and the public was naturally very concerned as to where the FLQ might strike next. It was certainly an unpleasant situation. The police were unable to report any progress in finding the kidnappers. The government of Québec was feeling the pressure to make a deal with the FLQ. The air was full of rumours, some of which were spread (I do not say invented) by ministers in the federal government. Unpleasant as all this was, it did not amount to the apprehended insurrection against which the federal government was invoking the War Measures Act and the use of extraordinary powers.

Mr. Turner, the Minister of Justice, implied that the government had information it could not disclose. "It is my hope," he told the House of Commons, "that some day the full details of the intelligence upon which the government acted can be made public, because until that day comes the people of Canada will not be able fully to appraise the course of action which has been taken by the government." Mr. Trudeau, however, insisted that all the facts upon which the government had based its use of the Act were public knowledge. Clearly Mr. Turner and Mr. Trudeau were not both right.

Before the end of 1970, it was plain that the kidnappings of Cross and Laporte were the uncoordinated work of two small groups of terrorists. Years later on November 2, 1977 in the House of Commons, Mr. Trudeau made his frankest and most illuminating public comment on the October Crisis: "at the time of the October 1970 events the police had to throw a very wide net indeed and arrest many people who were apparently guilty of nothing because the police were misinformed."

Certainly our government has a right, indeed a duty, to protect the country and its institutions against armed threats from within and without. If a government fears an insurrection even though it has no conclusive proof, it can be criticized for lack of information, but it ought not wait until an actual insurrection occurs before taking reasonable precautions. We can only guess whether or not the Prime Minister really feared an insurrection in 1970—he never said flatly that there was an apprehended insurrection—but the events of October showed clearly how easy it is in Canada for a government to have a suspension of civil liberties on assertions of an apprehended insurrection, without giving Parliament or the Canadian people any factual justification or subsequent accounting. Requests for a formal inquiry into the events of October 1970 have been rejected by the Prime Minister as unnecessary.

The plain truth is that most Canadians did not care whether or not there really was an apprehended insurrection. They did not like what was going on in Québec and they approved of their federal government taking strong measures to deal with the situation; if the government had no tools other than the War Measures Act, then by all means let the government use it. To many if not most Canadians any questioning of the invocation of the Act was unpatriotic even before the murder of Pierre Laporte.

What is most significant and revealing is not that the government of the day resorted to such a measure—another government might have done that, too—but that in a state of concern the public enthusiastically approved the measure, and since then has never wanted any accounting for either the claim of an apprehended insurrection or the behaviour of security and police forces towards the citizens whose basic legal rights were suspended.

At the time I was surprised when the government resorted to the War Measures Act, as I had no reason to suspect, after government briefings, that we were confronted by anything more than the unco-ordinated activities of ruthless terrorist cells; I was shocked by what seemed to he the Canadian public's disregard of the importance of time-honoured rights. It was distressingly clear that most Canadians, when worried, did not value the civil liberties of other Canadians. And when feelings were running strongly our journalists, with few excep-tions, did not care enough to question what was happening. Ron Haggart, to his great credit, was one of those who did. In such circum-stances politicians, with few exceptions, also become very prudent: they too were generally not prepared to go against the fervent emotions of their constituents.

A common form of apology was that the War Measures Act was the only means the government had of restoring order in Québec and bringing the terrorists to justice. Haggart and Golden emphasize in *Rumours of war* that the war measures regulations did not give the police any methods of detection that would not normally be available; they simply provided the power to intern. It may be said that the invoca-tion of the Act was necessary to restore order, but was it the invocation of the Act or the shock of Pierre Laporte's murder that quieted things down in Québec? It may be said that this measure must be given credit for dampening subsequent terrorism in Québec, but that statement would be difficult to accept since such measures have not discouraged terrorists in other countries. Whatever the answer, our country is on a very slippery slope if the government is allowed to justify the suspen-sion of basic civil liberties by pretending that the state is threatened by insurrection.

One can only guess whether a future government would be more or less likely to resort to the War Measures Act in comparable circum-stances. Journalists then might well ask more questions or attack the suspension of traditional liberties and politicians, recalling the events lucidly described and analyzed in *Rumours of war,* might resist the gov-ernment. Nevertheless, October 1970 showed how readily Canadians will back arbitrary action to deal with something they dislike and fear.

Terrorism in Québec, culminating in the kidnappings of 1970, and the overall increase in the number of violent crimes have strengthened the demand for law and order in Canada. The force of that demand is apparent in the vigorous support for capital punishment and concern about methods used to enforce the law is now much weaker. A climate of mounting violence in our society is not healthy for civil liberties.

Did the events of 1970 encourage some members of our security forces to resort subsequently to illegal methods in the performance of their duties? The McDonald Commission may or may not answer that question with authority when it has completed its work. It does seem to me, however, that the free hand given in Québec in 1970 and the lack of any accounting as to how that free hand was used with the exception of statistics concerning the number of arrests and charges laid would create the impression in the minds of some policemen operating in Québec that illegal methods could be used where separatists were involved, and that those who used such methods would be protected.

Citizens who value civil liberties can derive some encouragement from the widespread concern about allegedly illegal security operations which led the government to appoint the McDonald Commission. Opposition members of Parliament pursued the issue despite complaints that they were smearing the RCMP. It is fortunate that this issue of arbitrary and illegal security measures has come to the fore in an atmosphere of relative emotional calm; unless the calm is broken we have a fair chance that the findings and recommendations of the Commission will be considered by the government, Parliament and public with some degree of dispassion. We may then have the opportunity to formulate rules and guidelines for security operations which are consistent with a concern for civil liberties.

This would be civilized progress, but it would still be limited progress. Although appropriate guidelines for security operations are important, we cannot reasonably hope to protect the individual from arbitrary official behaviour by written rules or laws alone. Our present Bill of Rights makes provision for a War Measures Act or its equivalent, and any bill of rights likely to be enshrined in our constitution will have to do the same. Civil liberties in Canada will therefore continue to depend basically upon the importance Canadians attach to them and upon our willingness to defend them even in times of stress. In our search for protection from violence we must recognize that arbitrary abrogation of individual rights weakens rather than strengthens social order. *Rumours of war* helps us to understand this and tells us something about ourselves we must not be allowed to forget.

"It was not just Pierre Trudeau.
It was all of us."

Thomas R. Berger

◆

EDITORS' NOTES
This anthology begins with an overview of the history of freedoms in
Canada prior to October 1970 written by Thomas Berger. In 1981, he pub-
lished his views, in hindsight, on the events of October 1970.

◆

Was there any evidence at all that an insurrection in Quebec was
imminent? Two men had been kidnapped—by two different groups
who might or might not be closely linked. Public figures in Quebec,
who had been making inflammatory speeches for years, were still
making inflammatory speeches. There had been meetings. Students
had publicly demonstrated their support for the FLQ, but it was not the
first time that students in Quebec or elsewhere had supported radical
or dubious causes. Did this kind of evidence justify a state of siege?

On October 23, Trudeau, in answer to questions, offered the House
his justification for invoking the War Measures Act:

> The first fact was that there had been kidnappings of two very important
> people in Canada and that they were being held for ransom under threat
> of death. The second was that the government of the province of Quebec
> and the authorities of the City of Montreal asked the federal government
> to permit the use of exceptional measures because, in their own words, a
> state of apprehended insurrection existed. The third reason was our assess-
> ment of all the surrounding facts, which are known to the country by
> now—the state of confusion that existed in the province of Quebec in
> regard to these matters.

That was the evidence that the head of the government, in a considered answer, relied upon. Trudeau referred as well to the fact that "a great quantity of dynamite has been stolen in Quebec during the last year and not recovered, that there is a great quantity . . . of rifles and small arms that have disappeared." Trudeau cannot be accused of withholding evidence. "The facts that are known to the House," he said, "are the facts on which we acted and it is on that that we stand." The evidence that has come to light since 1970 supports Trudeau's contention that the House had all the information available to the government at the time. The disclosures made since 1970 about some of the activities of the RCMP, while disturbing, do not appear to have been known to the federal cabinet in 1970.

There had been an insurrection against the regime at Quebec City in the past—a real insurrection, in 1837, Louis-Joseph Papineau had inspired an armed uprising against the government of Lower Canada, and there were armed clashes between the rebels and British troops. At St. Charles and St. Eustache, the rebels had been defeated. There were many casualties. One of the rebels who was killed was Dr. Jean Chenier. Thousands were imprisoned. Martial law was declared. The rebellion was renewed in 1838, and crushed again. There were grounds for extraordinary measures then. But the FLQ, unlike Papineau, Chenier, and the rebels of 1837-38, had no organized popular following, no rational scheme for establishing a new order in Quebec, and no intention of engaging the Canadian armed forces or the police in open conflict.

There was no basis for claiming that an insurrection was imminent in 1970. Robert Stanfield, leader of the Conservative party during the October Crisis, supported the government then. But, in June, 1979, he wrote that events in Quebec at the time "did not amount to the apprehended insurrection against which the Federal Government was invoking the War Measures Act and the use of extraordinary powers." Few would argue with this verdict. Why, then, would anyone, considering the evidence, have reached any other conclusion in 1970?

Clearly, Trudeau and his colleagues felt that they had to do something. But when every allowance has been made for the difficulties they had in assessing what was really happening—given the two kidnappings, the fiery statements of Quebec radicals, and the personal dilemma the Laporte kidnapping presented for many of them—it is impossible to avoid the conclusion that, given "the state of confusion that existed in the province of Quebec," Trudeau and his colleagues decided to assert the federal power and authority in a definitive way. Terrorists and terrorism would not shake them. The strength of the state had to he demonstrated. (...)

Many politicians—together with other citizens—believe that, in a political crisis, the ordinary rules of debate must be suspended, and those who seek to take advantage of the right to criticize must be treated as if they wished to accomplish the destruction of the state. All doubts about the wisdom of government action must be vanquished if the enemies of the state are to be vanquished.

It is not, however, upon the assumption of extraordinary governmental powers that the safety of the state depends, but upon the conviction of the people that the right to dissent is essential to the life and health of the state. Firmness is better shown—and often greater courage is required to show firmness—in the defence of civil liberties, by reminding the electorate of the need to distinguish between sedition and dissent, and of the difference between criminal acts established by evidence and guilt by association.

The proclamation by Trudeau's government of the War Measures Act was an affirmation of the will to govern against an attempt by terrorists to prove that our institutions are impotent. The use of terrorism is lamentably widespread. By acts of terrorism, terrorists try to shake the will of those who govern—to make the state tremble. Against this threat, Trudeau affirmed the federal government's determination to deal decisively with subversive activities. But was it necessary to turn two kidnappings into a seditious conspiracy, a conspiracy of proportions so threatening that it could be checked only by the abrogation of civil liberties throughout Canada? Would not a resolute and uncompromising defence of civil liberties have served the nation better? The government certainly had, and should have assured the public that it knew it had, ample power and the necessary means to capture the kidnappers. I think that such actions would have demonstrated the strength of the nation and of its Constitution more surely than the abrogation of the citizen's rights. Our leaders should have called for patience and restraint, not for extraordinary measures to augment the already formidable powers of the government and the police. (...)

Study of the October Crisis demonstrates that a prime minister, whose earlier career had been devoted to defending the rights of dis-

180 ◆ TRUDEAU'S DARKEST HOUR

senters, could himself become the instrument of large-scale arrests and the repression of dissent, simply because the powers to do so are available to the persons elected to govern us. Our Constitution should reflect a faith in laws, not in those who govern; it should reflect a faith in fundamental freedoms, not a willingness to give the persons who govern us the power to repeal them.

Pierre Trudeau, before he entered Parliament, provided compelling arguments for the entrenchment of fundamental freedoms and for placing limits on police power. In high office, in October, 1970, he provided compelling evidence why these freedoms should be entrenched. But it was not just Pierre Trudeau, it was all of us. The October Crisis was a crucible. During that period, unnamed fears that lie just beneath our conscious minds were suddenly fused into one clear certainty to which everyone clung. For a moment, Canadians banished all their uncertainties related in one way or another to the crisis by exorcising the FLQ. Questions about the rights of all kinds of dissenters, French or English, were ignored in a glorious act of self-indulgent wrath. Canadian unity had never been more fervently felt nor more stridently upheld by so many.

"Trudeau's Target was the affluent dilettantes of revolutionary violence."

Desmond Morton

◆

EDITORS' NOTES
According to historian Desmond Morton, as early as 1967 after Charles de Gaulle made his "Vive le Québec libre" speech on July 24 from the Montreal City Hall, shocked English Canadians jumped aboard the Pierre Trudeau bandwagon electing him as prime minister in 1968 with the strongest majority the House of Commons had known since 1963. Trudeau's mission was clear: to restore Canada's confidence.

Of all the "separatists," as Trudeau liked to call them, he was mainly out to get the "affluent dilettantes," "coffee table revolutionaries," "artists, students and connoisseurs of radical chic." That was his goal in October 1970, in Desmond Morton's opinion, and not the "two frightened little bands of terrorists."

He needed the police to do that. Reg Whitaker in Chapter 5, "Deploying the War Measures," points out that the RCMP was ready. He also needed an army. According to Dan Loomis in the same chapter, the army had been reengineered with exactly that goal in mind. The prime minister also had to prime himself and his government, and he did so on several occasions and specifically on May 5, 1970, just one week after the Parti Québécois had obtained twenty-three percent of the popular vote and elected seven members to the Quebec National Assembly. [1] On that day in May 1970, Trudeau chaired a government committee that looked into the possibility of invoking "war measures." [2]

Recourse to state violence was not new to Trudeau. He often referred to arrests "in the middle of the night" as the article by Cruickshank in

---

1. Several months earlier, on October 18, 1969, in his "Fini les folies" speech, Trudeau had described the Parti Québécois as nothing more than a "particule" that would never get anybody elected. The results of the April 29 election must have been a rude awakening for him.

2. Louis Fournier, *FLQ, Histoire d'un mouvement clandestin*, 1998, p. 250.

Chapter 6, "Nobody Was Left Unscathed," shows. Other public statements left no doubt about his intentions. In 1968, during an election speech in Quebec's Abitibi region, he railed the "separatists" saying, *"Vous allez vous faire mal,"* "You're going to hurt yourselves." Then in 1969 before some three thousand militant Liberals, he attacked the confusion in people's minds, disorder in the streets, and the influence of Quebec ideas up to the highest echelons of the Quebec civil service and among French-speaking journalists. "We will not allow our country to be divided, either from within or from outside," he shouted. Speaking directly to journalists at Radio-Canada, among whom he claimed that separatism had become a "mental illness," he warned that "if necessary we'll just shut the place down!" He concluded that tirade with "Fini les folies!" which could be translated as the "the fun is over."

The very next day, on October 19, on Radio-Canada's leading public affairs program *Format 30*, Trudeau abrasively interrupted host Louis Martin, who had reproached the prime minister for his impatience towards his "separatist" opponents. He declared in English on the French-language network, "You haven't seen anything yet."

It was almost exactly one year later that he replied to a CBC reporter, who was also worried, with his famous "Just watch me." His so-called "affluent dilettantes" and their friends could not say they hadn't been warned.

Desmond Morton is a Canadian historian who specializes in the history of the Canadian military. Born in Calgary in 1937, he is the son of a Brigadier General, and the grandson of a General. A graduate of the Collège militaire royal de St-Jean and The Royal Military College of Canada and a Rhodes Scholar, he studied at Oxford and the London School of Economics. He spent ten years in the Canadian Army prior to beginning his teaching career. He taught at the University of Toronto and McGill University and is the author of over thirty-five books on Canada. In 1996, he was made an Officer of the Order of Canada and is a Fellow of the Royal Society of Canada. Here is an excerpt from *A Military History of Canada*, first published in 1985.[3]

◆

On February 1, 1968, unification of the armed forces formally took effect. Few Canadians cared. (…)

---

3. Desmond Morton, *A Military History of Canada*, Hurtig Publishers, Edmonton 1985; reproduced with permission from McGill/Queen's University Press.

Above all, Canadians worried about Quebec. The Centennial mood had been lifted by the glittering triumph of Expo 67; it had been shattered when Montrealers cheered Charles de Gaulle's cry of "*Vive le Québec libre.*"

Suddenly the resolution of every Canadian problem seemed bound up in the enigmatic personality of Pierre Elliott Trudeau. (...)

On June 26, he headed the first majority Liberal government since 1957. The enigma remained. As a prank in wartime Montreal, he had allegedly dressed in a "Nazi" uniform. In 1963 he had voted NDP in protest at Pearson's nuclear change of heart. Trudeau admired such military virtues as courage and fitness but he had Mackenzie King's distaste for military minds. (...) He devised elaborate machinery for decision-making but remained endlessly indecisive.

Defence was a logical place for the new rational decision-making to start. Analysts like John Gellner had long complained that Ottawa made defence policy backwards, choosing weapons and then finding roles for them. The Trudeau system made no such elementary error. On April 3, 1969, underlining the new importance of his office, the prime minister issued Canada's defence priorities:

(a)   the surveillance of our territory and coastline—i.e., the protection of our sovereignty;
(b)   the defence of North America in co-operation with United States forces;
(c)   the fulfillment of such NATO commitments as maybe agreed upon;
(d)   the performance of such international peacekeeping roles as we may from time to time assume.

Trudeau had turned the Hellyer priorities of 1964 upside down. Hellyer's lowest concern had been "providing for certain aspects of security and protection within Canada"; as for "surveillance," it surged to the top. (...)

In 1970, Cadieux's successor, Donald Macdonald, explained that the forces' new priority would be guarding Canadian sovereignty and contributing to "the social and economic development of Canada." (...) (His) 1970 white paper, *Defence in the Seventies*, cautiously included internal security in the task of defending sovereignty. Memories of aid to the civil power had faded but Canadian television viewers were familiar with American soldiers, helmeted and armed, playing their role in the "long hot summers" of the 1960s. British troops had been dragged into the communal violence of Northern Ireland while French soldiers and paramilitary police had recaptured Paris's Left Bank in the violent May Days of 1968. Violence in the United States, Trudeau warned a Queen's University audience in 1969, could easily spill into Canada.

In fact, violence was quite indigenous. Mailbox bombings earlier in the decade had left one military explosives expert crippled for life. In 1969, after Montreal police went on strike, youths chanted revolutionary slogans as they attacked an English-owned bus company. As crowds looted downtown Montreal stores, troops rushed from Valcartier. A year later, on October 5, 1970, a group calling itself the Quebec Liberation Front kidnapped the British trade commissioner in Montreal. Five days later, another FLQ cell kidnapped the Quebec labour minister, Pierre Laporte. Artists, students, and connoisseurs of radical chic promptly lionized the kidnappers. Prominent critics of Robert Bourassa's provincial government met, debated the crisis, and offered themselves as a more competent and conciliatory administration.

Pierre Elliott Trudeau was not amused. On October 14, two days after Laporte was seized, he ordered troops to Ottawa to guard public buildings and prominent politicians. On October 15, the Quebec premier formally requisitioned aid to the civil power: battalions of the Royal 22e Régiment, posted just north of Montreal, responded at once. Next morning, at 4 a.m., "after consideration of all the facts and particularly letters received from the Prime Minister of Quebec and the authorities of the city of Montreal, reporting a state of apprehended insurrection," Trudeau invoked the War Measures Act.

It was unprecedented. On the basis of facts then and revealed later, it was unjustified. It was also a brilliant success. Shock was the best safeguard against bloodshed. Trudeau's target was not two frightened little bands of terrorists, one of which soon strangled its helpless victim: it was the affluent dilettantes of revolutionary violence, cheering on the anonymous heroes of the FLQ. The proclamation of the War Measures Act and the thousands of grim troops pouring into Montreal froze the cheers, dispersed the coffee-table revolutionaries, and left them frightened and isolated while the police rounded up suspects whose offence, if any, was dreaming of blood in the streets.

For the Canadian armed forces, the October crisis was an ambiguous experience. It was an exciting test of staff procedures, communications systems, and troops. Few had ever shared in operations of such magnitude. (…) Thoughtful officers also knew that Trudeau's "Priority One," surveillance of our territory, now posed a greater danger than any other potential role. By proclaiming emergency powers, the prime minister had staked not only his own prestige but that of the armed forces on a satisfactory outcome. In 1972, when the government claimed that it would use the forces again, the Conservative defence critic, Michael Forrestal, offered a prudent warning: "the deliberate use of the military to enforce the will of one group of Canadians over the will of another group of Canadians is detrimental to the credibility of the armed forces." No party was willing to suggest an alternative.

"Trudeau's, Mackasey's and Lalonde's horrific jack-boot approach to their own people."

Hugh Segal

◆

EDITORS' NOTES
Hugh Segal is a well-known political personality. This "Red Tory" originally from Montreal was appointed to the Senate in 2005 by Liberal Prime Minister Paul Martin to represent the Ontario Senatorial Designation of Kingston-Frontenac-Leeds. He had earlier been advisor to Ontario Premier Bill Davis and to Prime Minister Brian Mulroney. He has also written extensively about politics and published a book of memories and reflections entitled *No Surrender* in 1996.

Hugh Segal was a twenty-year-old University of Ottawa history student when the war measures were imposed. As president of the Students' Federation, he managed to make his "moderate" position prevail and to convince students to be confident in, and to give the benefit of the doubt to, the government. "Surely it is not too much to ask of a free people to just once assume that their government cannot disclose all the facts, and must be supported pending the release of the pertinent details." At that time, he called it "a national act of faith in the Trudeau Government."

He soon became disenchanted. Things got out of control and campuses began to feel the weight of censorship. "Posters were being torn," "student councils were called by their printers, several minutes before the RCMP were called by the same printers." Most of all, however, he realized that the government had no intention of justifying its actions: "the government in Ottawa wasn't interested in any answers." That attitude of the Trudeau government effectively delegitimized his position as a "moderate" and he understood it perfectly. "The battle was clearly lost," he wrote, disillusioned. "A generation that desired so deeply to trust was alienated so completely by the man they helped make Prime Minister of Canada." He made these thoughts clear as early as November 1970 in the pamphlet he helped produce *Strong and Free, A Response to the War Measures*, excerpts of which are provided in Chapter 7.

Twenty-five years later he revisited the crisis in *No Surrender* and was even more indignant about what had been done. He was incensed about the methods used by the government, the "jack-boot approach," which inevitably reminded the former history student of the darkest years of a very dark century. He was angry at seeing political leaders betray the social, intellectual, and trade union circles from whence they came, but also seeing them betray "their own people," who had shown such confidence in them. He was also upset at seeing the injurious impact that the operation launched that "fateful Friday morning" would have on the evolution of the constitutional relationship between Quebec and the rest of Canada.

Hugh Segal's thoughts on the war measures are part of his chapter in *No Surrender* entitled "The loss of innocence," both his and that of an entire country.[1]

◆

There is, however, a truly dark side to the power of the state, and it was revealed in October 1970 when Pierre Trudeau and his minister of Justice, John Turner, brought in the War Measures Act. Armoured personnel carriers moved troops around our campus, making an intimidating show of force. Students and faculty who were members of René Lévesque's Parti Québécois were detained for no apparent reason. Offices were raided by well-meaning but essentially ill-informed police. Membership lists were taken.

Members of the PQ on campus were detained for questioning, some for more than a day. I heard later that John Robarts was terribly offended when he found out that, while essentially enforced in Quebec, the act applied to the whole country and could have been used just as easily to round up dissident students at York. No one to my knowledge was beaten or manhandled in any way and no one conveniently disappeared as might have happened in countries like Argentina, but it became clear that even in a society as fundamentally kind and decent as our own, you can find yourself in difficulty, mostly unwittingly, if you give the wrong kinds of power to police officers and soldiers not trained to deal with complex legal situations.

I called Bob Stanfield's office and spoke to his appointment secretary, Murray Coolican, about the detained students. Stanfield raised questions

1. Hugh Segal, No Surrender, *Reflections of a Happy Warrior in the Tory Crusade*, Toronto, HarperCollins Publishers Ltd. 1996.

in the House, asking the solicitor-general why they were being held, only to get the standard response of "I want to thank the Leader of the Opposition for the question. I'll look into the matter." (...)

I realized that it is a mistake to assume that Canadians intrinsically respect minority rights and civil liberties and are prepared to go to battle for them. If the waterhole gets smaller, the animals start to look at each other in a different way, which we saw with the Japanese and the other internees during the Second World War. We can become uncivil to each other *in extremis.*

For the vast majority of Canadians, the War Measures Act was not a personal threat and they were prepared to give *carte blanche* to the government in view of the alleged facts. (...)

Canadians have a noble commitment to order, but the flip side is that there is little evidence to suggest that they have as great a commitment to democracy as the British and Americans have. There has rarely been any significant outcry against abuse of authority, whether through the use of troops against striking unionists in Winnipeg, the use of a quasi-military force against strikers in southwestern Ontario, or the imposition of the War Measures Act by Pierre Trudeau.

Imagine an American president, faced with a secessionist movement in Texas, suspending clear across the country all the civil liberties and rights protected by the U.S. constitution. There would be uproar in the streets and a move for impeachment for violating democratic principles. Yet here in Canada in October 1970, four hundred people were arrested without charge in the middle of the night, held in jail for days with not one of them ever charged with so much as double parking, with police officers deciding who was a danger to the state, and with civil liberties— including the right to free assembly, the right to free speech, and other fundamental rights—suspended across the land.

This was bad government, pure and simple. It was panic on the part of Bourassa and, in my view, the worst kind of fascist totalitarianism on the part of Trudeau, Bryce Mackasey in Labour, and Marc Lalonde, the prime minister's principal secretary, a horrific jack-boot approach to their own people they felt comfortable taking because they had been elected in 1968 on the premise that they were going to "handle" French Canada. They were encouraged by the worst anti-French bigots outside Quebec because Trudeau stood with courage the day of the St.-Jean-Baptiste Day parade dodging flying bottles. Their mandate was to handle "those people," and if that meant calling out the army, so be it.

Certainly it was unacceptable that law enforcement agencies were unable to deal with FLQ cells that did, in fact, murder a minister of the Crown and did endorse the broad use of bombings, shootings, and other acts of violence to achieve political ends. It betrayed a lack of police intelligence on the ground and a lack of police capacity, maturity, and judgment in Quebec that we have yet to outgrow. The idea of British diplomats being kidnapped, cabinet ministers being abducted and murdered, and terrorists getting air time on radio is not the sense of order we believe in. But how order is achieved and what force is used when there is a breakdown of order are the measures of civility in society.

The War Measures Act was not the only vehicle available to the authorities. Marshal law could have been imposed. The army could have been invited in, as it was in Oka when the police were clearly overwhelmed. Any premier has the right under the constitution to request military aid to the civil power, but in that circumstance there still is a civil power, there still is a constitution, a Bill of Rights, habeas corpus, due process, and the law. All of that was wiped away, allowing police to arrest people without having any idea what they were to be charged with or without any reasonable suspicion of wrong-doing. They were arrested because they were on lists.

Bryce Mackasey implied in the House "that they would divulge the information that made them do it." To date, scholars have found nothing to substantiate even the hint of an insurrection. It is now commonly believed that the letters sent by Premier Bourassa and Montreal's mayor, Jean Drapeau, were written by, and carried to them, by Marc Lalonde.

The federal cabinet argued at the time that the police were too tired, overwhelmed, and needed the War Measures Act to help. But the RCMP didn't ask for it, the military didn't ask for it, the local police never asked for it. Politicians made the decision. Why? The only conclusion is that someone decided that it was appropriate to use the apparatus of the state to settle the score, which is the kind of serious miscarriage of democracy that citizens pay a price for.

This was the end of my political innocence. I began to understand that there are consequences to the rhetoric of arrogance and the consequences can be very unpleasant indeed. This is still a peaceable kingdom and a wonderful society. I remain a great supporter of the national defence department, but not for its use against our own people. When citizens see armoured vehicles patrolling on a campus in the centre of Ottawa, they know that something has gone terribly wrong.

My vitriolic dislike for Pierre Trudeau's policies emerged during this period. I developed an intense dislike for his arrogance, his condescension, and his readiness to impose his will even on people with whom he had argued across the kitchen table for twenty-five years. That act of rank repression shaped in me a profound and fundamental distrust of what federal Liberals had done constitutionally and a sense that our constitutional difficulties even today are very much the product of events that transpired more than twenty years ago. This was the point of departure and legitimacy for more extreme nationalism. Those who went on to advance the separatist cause in Quebec only reflected in a more extreme way the obvious conclusions the War Measures Act would have imposed on any thoughtful nationalist who wondered about his or her ability to defend Quebec's legitimate interests within Canada.

On campus, the result was that many French-Canadians who didn't take politics seriously started taking politics very seriously indeed. I saw an entire generation develop a sense of despair and a sense that those guilty of having a view outside the mainstream, especially in Quebec, might no longer expect the civility our society is said to embrace.

"[That] had not been what my long friendship with Trudeau had led me to expect."

Ramsay Cook

◆

EDITORS' NOTES

George Ramsay Cook was born in Manitoba in 1931. As a historian and academic, Cook was very familiar with Quebec and had devoted several books to it. He was also a friend and admirer of Pierre Elliott Trudeau and he supported his efforts to maintain "national unity."

He was nonetheless opposed to war measures out of principle. His master's thesis entitled "Canadian liberalism in wartime", which he defended at Queen's University in 1955, dealt with the subject. The War Measures Act shocked him and he found it totally unacceptable: "I believed it should long since have been erased from the Statute books." He was thus understandably shocked to see soldiers in Montreal in October 1970: "The sight of armed soldiers on the streets of downtown Montreal—not a great many, but some—left me depressed." He admitted that throughout that crisis he fell into "emotional turmoil and intellectual confusion." He felt torn both as a former New Democrat and as an admirer of the NDP for its stalwart defence of freedoms.

He participated in a university debate and publicly stated, "What, I asked, could justify the arrest of the popular singer Pauline Julien?" He signed a petition with other personalities but otherwise remained discreet in his opposition. "I lapsed into silence," he wrote, fearing that he might hinder Trudeau in his combat against those who backed Quebec, but he also "feared that [his] friendship with Trudeau hung in the balance."

When he publicly took a stance with others in the document *Strong and Free* (Chapter 7.3), he received a "long letter" from Jim Davey, a Strategic Operations official, who made it very clear to him that the positions he was taking were being closely monitored by people at the top. In that letter, Davey was indignant that some people claimed that Trudeau had "some ulterior motive." He also insisted that mass demonstrations in the streets of Montreal had to be avoided—the Kent State University shooting was still fresh in people's minds—and that no "martyrs" to the Quebec cause should be provided.

Davey failed to convince Cook. "I remain a skeptic," he concluded. Ramsay Cook published his book of memories in 2006, several years after Trudeau had passed away.[1] Trudeau was thus spared from having to read that some people considered that their friendship with, and admiration for, the former prime minister had suffered during that "doleful October" crisis.

◆

In response to a reported "apprehended insurrection," [Trudeau] had done what he had believed necessary: proclaimed the War Measures Act. Consequently, the "apprehended" never become "real." Could it have? How can anyone know if the "perceived" insurrection had been squelched? That, in my mind, had always been the essential defect of the War Measures Act; it left "apprehended" undefined. What a government "apprehends" as insurrection may look less threatening to others. The controversy over the October Crisis will never end, since there will always be different assessments of the relationship between "apprehended" and "real" insurrection. On that point, though no one articulated it, there was no agreement when the prime minister and my other friends met and debated on the night before my thirty-ninth birthday.

In January 1971, I received a long letter from Jim Davey who, though I was unaware of it at the time, directed the Strategic Operations Centre that devised and implemented the federal government's response to the crisis. Davey said he had seen my name on a pamphlet criticizing the use of the War Measures Act and wondered if that represented my views. The pamphlet, entitled *Strong and Free: A Response to the War Measures Act*,[2] contained eleven brief articles that questioned, in fairly measured terms, the Trudeau government's action. Over sixty highly respectable citizens, including Claude Bissell, Lloyd Axworthy, Dalton Camp, Pauline Jewett, and Gordon Fairweather, signed it. Not surprisingly, those who suggested that the government had some ulterior motive in invoking the War Measures Act—an idea Davey pronounced "preposterous"—especially irritated him. He insisted that the depth of

1. Ramsay Cook, *The Teeth of Time: Remembering Pierre Elliott Trudeau*, Montréal, Itahaca, McGill/Queen's University Press 2006.
2. See chapter 7.3

the crisis in Quebec, a crisis that was not simply the FLQ actions but was a profound crisis of authority, had to be understood very broadly. Only a powerful defence of the rule of law, of legitimate authority, could shore up a deteriorating situation and prevent the rot from spreading. He offered a revealing parallel.

But what is the balance sheet of the Quebec crisis? Over 400 people were arrested and put in prison for various periods of time, which is clearly something that no one is very happy about. But there were no people killed in the street, and there are no martyrs to the Quebec cause, where there might well have been. You, as a historian, know very well what would be the symbolic importance of the four or five CEGEP kids [community college students] "killed in the cause of Quebec." Remember what happened after four such kids were killed at Kent State. Over 400 people were arrested and several have complained of various kinds of abuse. That kind of treatment is not condoned, but what is remarkable is that during this very tense situation the control of the authorities and the police was such that there was not considerably more.

I knew that Trudeau had been concerned with the possibility that social unrest might lead to the same kind of violent situation that other countries were experiencing. He had questioned me about unrest in the United States. He had read a piece I wrote in *Le Devoir* commenting on Hannah Arendt's *On Violence*. Quebec in the 1960s and 1970s was in a state of convulsion whose outcome was unpredictable. The FLQ crisis demonstrated that. But was the War Measures Act the best, the only possible emergency response? I replied to Davey saying that I understood that my information about the crisis in Quebec might be deficient and that the seriousness of the situation required a firm response. But the powers provided by the War Measures Act were almost inevitable invitations to abuse. Did the magnitude of the threat equal the magnitude of the response? I needed more evidence. Not a harsh word was exchanged, nor did I feel any pain in my arm. (...)

During the next few weeks, and since, I have thought a great deal about the determined defence that Trudeau and Davey offered for the federal government's response to the FLQ terror. Repeatedly I have re-examined the main arguments. I accepted their assessment of the seriousness of the challenge which the three levels of government had faced, and I thought that, for an outsider, I knew Quebec very well. But had the War Measures Act been the only recourse? Had special legislation with more limited provisions for search and arrest been given thorough consideration? Marc Lalonde, in the final issue of *Cité libre* (Fall 2000), said that cabinet documents revealed that Trudeau, when first faced with the proposal that the War Measures Act be proclaimed, maintained that existing laws were sufficient. Special legislation also was considered but was rejected because its rapid passage was too uncertain. In the end, the cabinet decided to resort to the War Measures Act and Trudeau agreed, but he "certainly wasn't the one who pushed for it."

The arbitrary powers provided by the War Measures Act unfortunately did not lead to a quick resolution of the kidnappings: Laporte was murdered, and Cross remained in captivity until December. Doubtless, the threat of this arbitrary power made it plain to those playing with revolution that the consequences could be serious, and this helped to restore a sense of security to the streets of Montreal. There was no Kent State. Moreover, Trudeau had faced his critics, both in the House of Commons and in parts of the press, in a way that sharply contrasted with the King government's persistent avoidance of parliamentary scrutiny during the Second World War. Always willing to give Trudeau the benefit of the doubt, I nevertheless remained and remain a skeptic: measures not men, my master's thesis research had taught me.

Gérard Pelletier, a man utterly without an authoritarian bone in his body, went as far as I could go, sometimes. He called the policy he supported *la solution la moins mauvaise*. That, for me, summed up the October Crisis. But the politics of *la moins mauvaise* had not been what my long friendship with Trudeau had led me to expect.

CONCLUSION

In answer to two political kidnappings, the government of Pierre Elliott Trudeau invoked the War Measures Act on October 16 in the middle of the night. It thereby suspended the Constitution and all civil liberties and concentrated all power over the citizens of Canada in the hands of the prime minister, his inner cabinet, and his advisors. To justify the war measures, the Trudeau government claimed that there was a state of apprehended insurrection in Quebec. Yet the RCMP which was responsible for gathering intelligence on illegal activities in Quebec since 1963 and for finding the hostages and arresting the kidnappers had no such information and did not request war measures in order to accomplish the task before them. When the "apprehended insurrection" proved to be a flimsy argument, Pierre Trudeau and his chief political advisor Marc Lalonde floated a story in the media and political circles about a provisional government being formed by leading Quebec personalities who aimed to usurp power from Quebec's duly elected government led by Premier Robert Bourassa. That "meticulously concocted lie" was spread by a "sycophantic" press and it has remained in our collective memory as being based on fact. In short, the Trudeau government brazenly deceived the people of Canada and denied justice in October 1970.

The authors in this anthology do not mince their words in qualifying that denial of justice: "authoritarian," "totalitarian," "dictatorial," and even "fascist," with all that those words bring to mind. Hugh Segal described it as "something right out of Mein Kampf." Had the struggles of peoples throughout the centuries to conquer democratic rights and freedoms been of no avail?

The Canadian armed forces deployed 12,500 troops throughout Quebec with 7,500 in Montreal alone. Tens of thousands of provincial and municipal policemen overseen by RCMP were deployed. The combined police forces arrested, without warrant and often brutally, more than 450 Canadian citizens, held them incommunicado without charging them, without access to a lawyer and without possibility of bail. The same police forces searched and often broke into more than ten thousand homes. These arrests and searches were conducted against people whom the government had no legitimate reason to suspect of having taken part in any terrorist activities of the Front de libération du Québec. These are some examples of what John Conway describes as "state violence."

The Trudeau government acted as if it was faced with a civil war whereas only two people had been kidnapped by a handful of people who enjoyed the support of another handful of people. Tommy Douglas rightly called it "overkill on a gargantuan scale." What's more, the government deployed all of the means ordinarily used by dictatorships, with the exception of political assassinations and torture—though some stories bring that to mind too. These means included break-ins and arrests with loaded and pointed guns in the middle of the night; censorship and media-government collusion across Canada; and pro-government rallies for Canada.

Prime Minister Trudeau unleashed these forces simply by invoking two distinct laws. The first, known as *Aid to Civil Authorities*, is part of the *National Defence Act* and had been invoked quite often in the past without causing a controversy. The second, the *War Measures Act*, had never before been proclaimed in time of peace. Yet even in time of war, its use had been widely criticized because of its arbitrary nature and the abuses it inevitably engenders. Robert Fulford referred to its "monstrous regulations," and James Eayrs maintained that Canada's record of resorting to emergency measures shows them to have been "monuments to folly."

October 1970 falls unmistakably in that category. In the very early hours of October 16, with no requirement for evidence or authorization other than Prime Minister Trudeau's signature, the federal cabinet announced that there was a state of apprehended insurrection and proceeded to implement war measures. Former Conservative Leader Robert Stanfield points out that under the War Measures Act the government had no obligation to justify its use of power, either before or after invoking the act, and that it only had to answer to itself. No legal limits existed to curb the government's use or abuse of power. The legislative, executive, and judicial branches became one and the same thing with the government dictating the law, implementing it, and determining whether it was doing so correctly.

• • •

How did the Trudeau government define the "enemy" on whom it declared war on October 16, 1970? According to the Public Order Regulations issued by the government, the war measures applied not only to members of the FLQ and those associated with its activities, but also to persons who "advocate, promote or engage in the use of force or the commission of criminal offences as a means of accomplishing a governmental change within Canada…" This definition substantially widened the net.

Three days before invoking the War Measures Act, Prime Minister Trudeau granted his now famous "Just watch me" interview to reporters Tim Ralfe and Peter Reilly. He defined the enemy as "those who are committing violence against the total society and those who are trying to run the government through a parallel power by establishing their authority by kidnapping and blackmail (…) a parallel power which defies the elected power in this country." Both notions are vague and possibly very large in scope. After the war measures had been invoked, an exasperated Trudeau insisted to a skeptical Peter C. Newman that, "There is a conspiracy afoot. The ringleaders are Lévesque, Parizeau and Ryan, among others. This move toward a parallel power must be stopped (…) Unelected power is not moved by benign motives. (…) The plot to overthrow the government is real." Trudeau was using broad strokes to conceptualize the enemy so as to encompass such diverse political forces as those represented by the FLQ, René Lévesque, and Claude Ryan. Yet the War Measures Act had specified that the target was those promoting "the use of force" in order to accomplish "governmental change."

The best way to identify the targets of the war measures is to consider who in fact was arrested and detained and whose homes were searched. Professor Reg Whitaker established that an original list of 158 names was prepared mostly from RCMP files but also after consultation with Trudeau's ministers Gérard Pelletier and Jean Marchand. The Quebec police, particularly outside Montreal, were nonetheless "excessive in round-ups under special powers," so that those numbers were quickly exceeded. Authors in this book refer to a total of 465 detainees but since those police activities were and still are state secrets the truth will remain unknown until an official record of the arrests is made public. Another question remains unanswered: who expanded the original list and how did they proceed? If Whitaker's pattern were to hold, then it is possible that local police in consultation with local politicians took control of the list. A frightful hypothesis to say the least!

According to Professor John Conway, "those arrested, besides the core leadership of the local PQ associations, included not only those suspected of FLQ sympathy very broadly defined, but also labour leaders, community activists and organizers, separatists of all types, and those known for effective opposition to any of the three levels of government." He points out that not a single member of the FLQ was captured in the War Measures Act "arrest net."

In October 1970 Jacques Parizeau was president of the Parti Québécois Executive Committee and thus responsible for the party organization. In his unauthorized biography of Jacques Parizeau, CBC/Radio-Canada journalist Pierre Duchesne describes how the Parti Québécois was hit in 1970. "In Hull, the army struck hard, entering an unbelievable number of homes and apartments... In Trois-Rivières, in one night, the entire executive committee of the riding association was arrested and jailed... Parizeau learned that a riding association president received a visit from the police at 2 a.m. Before arresting him, the Sûreté du Québec forced his wife to undress and walk about nude in front of the police... Nobody was arrested in Drumondville... However, within days, the police had entered and searched more than 300 homes, most of the time in the middle of the night, with cars from all police forces mobilized and flashing their dome lights so that the red beams shone into all the windows in the neighbourhoods visited and terrorized the population... The PQ executive in Drummondville resigned and disappeared in the days that followed. Members tore up their cards and there was nobody left." [1]

It can be safely said therefore that the war measures were unleashed mainly against the independence movement led by the Parti Québécois, to which was added an array of other separatists and dissenters. The gap separating the official aims and the real targets is abysmal. The crisis became a pretext for massive repression and intimidation aimed at any political organization that contested the status quo. Robert Fulford con-

---

1. Pierre Duchesne, *Jacques Parizeau, Biographie 1930-1970, Tome 1, Le croisé*, Québec-Amérique, 2001, pp. 569-571 (our translation).

tended that the War Measures Act was a way to "throw an aura of crim-inality over all dissent to the left... of the PQ (and maybe to part of the PQ itself)." Those arrested experienced terror, degradation, and humilia-tion according to John Conway, who maintains that the main reason for the arrests was to warn people of the cost of their political convictions and actions. Jacques Parizeau recalled that the Parti Québécois lost half of its membership and forty ridings (out of 108) were left without any form of organization. "It almost wiped the party out," he confided, "and it left an indelible mark in some people's minds."

The stated goals of the Trudeau government were light years away from what the police and the army actually did at the government's behest. Yet since provisions in the War Measures Act dispense the Trudeau government from ever having to justify any action it took, we will never know why the Parti Québécois and other separatists became their primary targets.

• • •

Why did the Trudeau government launch such a massive operation against the independence movement? The answer to this question is complex and multifaceted.

The 1970 war measures operations required a high level of prepara-tion. It is impossible to deploy 12,500 troops without having a detailed strategy and substantial logistical support. Dan Loomis points out that as early as 1966 General Jean-Victor Allard had been planning a reorganization of the army so as to be able to defend the country against the internal threat of Quebec's possible secession. The reorganization was based on the "thesis of deterrence," which called for countering a man armed with a knife by mean of "a squad of soldiers with rifles pointed at his heart." According to Loomis, in 1969 the government and the military were "preparing for a showdown in Quebec."

From a police standpoint, the Secret Service of the RCMP, with three hundred officers in its Montreal detachment alone, was able to provide adequate intelligence that the FLQ was planning kidnappings and that James Cross and Pierre Laporte were potential targets. Yet the Secret Service did not consider the separatist movement as a whole to fall under its mandate with regard to monitoring practices of terrorism. According to a late 1969 RCMP report, the Parti Québécois "scrupu-lously adhered to an ethically and constitutionally correct approach to the Quebec question." Moreover, the RCMP had not documented any apprehended insurrection. Professor Reg Whitaker emphasizes in fact that, "The RCMP never asked for the War Measures Act, were not consulted as to its usefulness, and would have opposed it if they had been asked their opinion." This observation led Whitaker to conclude: "In invoking the powers of the War Measures Act, the Cabinet was answering formal requests from Quebec and Montreal, but in fact these requests were prompted by Ottawa. If they did not stem from the requirements of the federal police, whence did they come? (...) we can say with confidence that the decision came from the prime minister and his inner circle of Quebec ministers and advisors."

The Canadian Armed Forces had thus been prepared to meet the government's demand for aid to civil authorities, which would include protection of buildings and persons responsible for ensuring public order. On the other hand, the Secret Services were not prepared to arrest, detain, and interrogate people and to search people's homes on a large scale as permitted under the War Measures Act. What's more, they appear to have been reticent about acting in a way that might prevent them from achieving their primary goal of finding and freeing James Cross and Pierre Laporte and arresting their kidnappers.

The police were reticent about the War Measures Act as were some English-speaking cabinet ministers—Kierans and Jamieson in particular. In addition, the stories about an apprehended insurrection and a provisional government aimed at usurping power in Quebec were far from convincing. So how did the Trudeau government get away with it? The authors in this book answer that question.

Robert Fulford complained about the lack of effective protest. "Those silent men in the cabinet, and the many MPs who later sat with them had correctly judged the public mood. The people of Canada *wanted* their fellow citizens' rights denied." Trudeau cabinet minister Eric Kierans, who supported imposition of the war measures, candidly confessed thirty years later that he had made a "terrible mistake" and that he had given in to the "general hysteria outside and Trudeau's aura of control inside." Historian Jack Granatstein, who opposed the war measures, described the frightening nature of the crowd of five thousand students and faculty at a Rally for Canada at York University in Toronto. "The shouts from the students that interrupted my speech were frequent and hostile; the visceral hatred of the FLQ kidnappers and murders, and, as I interpreted it, of all Québécois was palpable." For Thomas Berger, Canadians had "banished all their uncertainties" and ignored questions regarding the rights of all kinds of dissenters in "a glorious act of self-indulgent wrath."

The wrath, fear, and hysteria they talk about were not simply directed at the small band of FLQ kidnappers but at a much broader and diffuse "enemy" of separatists, with Quebec as a whole not far behind. That is why the War Measures Act was adopted so easily and why the government enjoyed so much support afterwards. That also explains the formidable intimidation that cowed the small minority of opponents into silence or low-profile protest.

But more was required in the heart of the government apparatus in order to invoke the War Measures Act. Tommy Douglas argued that Trudeau hoped to crush the separatist movement and at the same time convince English Canadians that he was the strong man who could keep Quebec in its place. Historian Jack Granatstein, reporter Peter Reilly, and Member of Parliament David Macdonald all support Tommy Douglas's argument, but each in his own words. Trudeau was thus perceived by a very frightened English Canada—and he carefully cultivated the role—as the hero who would strike at the heart of separatism and leave it, if not in agony, at least in a state of powerlessness for the foreseeable future. English Canada was therefore ready, if not eager, for him to use whatever measures he judged necessary to eliminate an enemy that inspired fear among the people of Canada. And Trudeau was ready and eager to move.

The 1970 war measures were born out of a meeting of minds between a vast majority of English Canadians, who were overwhelming afraid of separatism defined in very broad terms in addition to being upset about the two kidnappings, and Pierre Elliott Trudeau and his closest advisors and ministers from Quebec, who held a long-standing, profound hatred for the independence movement. Being in government, they then had the powerful repressive tools they needed.

• • •

Jurist and lawyer Thomas R. Berger aptly raises the question of the contradiction between Pierre Trudeau, the defender of the rights of dissenters, and the prime minister of Canada who became "the instrument of large-scale arrests and dissent." This contradiction is even more glaring when considered in the light of Trudeau's 1948 letter from London cited in Chapter 2. In that published letter entitled *Reflections on a Democracy and its Variant,* he denounced the War Measures Act as a "tyrannical law" that "violated the fundamental principles of the society of equals" and supported Adrien Arcand's procedure against the Canadian Government. Adrien Arcand was an avowed Nazi and anti-Semite who repeatedly sided with the enemy. Yet just twenty-two years later the same Pierre Trudeau invoked the same War Measures Act, had more than 450 people arrested—none of whom had sided with the enemy—without charges, without bail, and without the right to speak to a lawyer, and had more than 10,000 homes entered and searched without warrants.

Trudeau admirers Max and Monique Nemni have written that while he was in twenties, Pierre Trudeau espoused fascist ideas.[2] Is it conceivable that, in October 1970, in his overwhelming desire to settle scores with his political opponents in Quebec, he reverted to the same ways and means that he had promoted as a young student in the 1940s? To answer that question, however, would require another book.

Political science professor Donald Smiley also raised the question of Trudeau's inconsistency as early as 1971. "During the October crisis and beyond, Mr. Trudeau's actions and utterances have belied all those fixed principles on which he formerly stood—the principles of individualism, rationalism and pragmatism. For individualism accords rather badly with the exercise of emergency powers. Rationalism is clearly contrary to a stance which suggests that the final test of the action of a government is the amount of public support forthcoming for that action. And pragmatism is based on an awareness of the mutual interpenetration of means and ends and a prudent relating of the two."[3]

Any attempt to reconcile the contradiction between Trudeau's thoughts and his actions leads inescapably to the conclusion that, in the end, his visceral hatred of separatism combined with English Canada's overwhelming fear of it, allowed him to put aside all other considerations. That is why the 1970 war measures will remain Trudeau's darkest hour.

2. Max and Monique Nemni, *Young Trudeau: 1919-1944, Son of Quebec, Father of Canada*, McClelland & Stewart, 2006.
3. Donald Smiley, "Consent, coercion and confederation," in *Power Corrupted*, edited by Abraham Rotstein, New Press, Toronto, 1971, p. 37.

BIBLIOGRAPHY

BERGER, Thomas R. *Fragile Freedoms: Human Rights and Dissent in Canada.* Toronto/Vancouver: Clarke, Irwin and Company Limited 1981.

BERGER, Thomas R. *One man's justice: A Life in the Law.* Vancouver/Toronto: Douglas and McIntyre; Seattle: University of Washington Press 2002.

BOTHWELL, Robert, DRUMMOND, Ian M., and English, John. *Canada, 1900-1945.* Toronto, Buffalo: University of Toronto Press 1987.

CLIPPINGDALE, Richard. *Robert Stanfield's Canada: Perspectives of the Best Prime Minister We never had.* Montreal/Kingston: McGill/Queen's 2008.

CONWAY, John F. *Debts to Pay. English Canada and Quebec from the Conquest to the Referendum.* Toronto: James Lorimer and Company, Publishers 1992 (2nd edition, 1997; 3rd edition, 2004).

COOK, Ramsay. *Canadian Liberalism in Wartime: A Study of the Defence of Canada Regulations and Some Canadian Attitudes to Civil Liberties in wartime.* M.A. Thesis, Queen's University, 1955.

COOK, Ramsay. *The teeth of time: remembering Pierre Elliott Trudeau.* Montreal, Ithaca: McGill-Queen's University Press 2006.

Crise d'octobre. Dossier de Presse. Tome I (6-22 octobre 1970). Tome II (27 octobre 1970-30 septembre 1980). Tome III (1 octobre 1980-16 mars 1988). Sherbrooke: Bibliothèque du séminaire de Sherbrooke 1988.

DUCHAÎNE, Jean-François. *Rapport sur les événements d'octobre* (2 vols). Gouvernement du Québec, Ministère de la Justice: 1980.

DUCHESNE, Pierre. *Jacques Parizeau. Tome I. Le Croisé 1930-1970.* Montréal: Éditions Québec Amérique 2001.

EAYRS, James. *Greenpeace and her Enemies.* Toronto: Anansi 1973.

Fournier, Louis. *FLQ. Histoire d'un movement clandestin.* Nouvelle edition, revue et augmentée. Outremont: Lanctôt éditeur 1998.

FULFORD, Robert. *Marshall Delaney at the movies: the contemporary world as seen on film.* P. Martin Associates 1974.

HAGGART, Ron and Golden, AUBREY E. *Rumours of War.* With a new introduction by Robert Stanfield. Toronto: James Lorimer & Company Publishers 1979. First published by New Press Toronto 1971.

JAMIESON, Don. *A World Unto Itself: The Political Memoirs of Don Jamieson.* Volume II. Edited by Carmelita McGrath. Breakwater Books, St John's Newfoundland: Don Jamieson 1991.

KIERANS, Eric. *Remembering.* With Walter Stewart. Toronto: Stoddart 2001.

LACHAPELLE, Guy. *Claude Ryan et la violence du pouvoir: Le Devoir et la Crise d'octobre 1970 ou le combat de journalists démocrates.* Préface de Jean-Claude Leclerc. Québec: Les Presses de l'Université Laval 2005.

LOOMIS, Dan G. *Not much glory: quelling the F.L.Q.* Toronto: Deneau 1984.

McLEOD, Thomas and McLEOD, Ian. *Tommy Douglas. The Road to Jerusalem.* Edmonton: Hurtig 1987.

MORTON, Desmond. *A Military History of Canada.* Edmonton: Hurtig Publishers 1985.

NEMNI, Max and Monique NEMNI. *Young Trudeau: 1919-1944, Son Quebec, Father of Canada.* Toronto: McClelland & Stewart 2006.

NEWMAN, Peter C. *Here be Dragons: Telling Tales of People, Passion and Power.* Toronto: McClelland and Stewart 2004.

Nick: A Montreal Life. Edited by Dave Bist. Introduction by Mordecai Richler. Caricatures by Aislin. Montreal: Véhicule Press 1998.

O'LEARY, Grattan. *Grattan O'Leary: recollections of people, press and politics.* Toronto: Macmillan of Canada 1977.

Power Corrupted: The October Crisis and The Repression of Quebec. Edited by Abraham Rotstein for the Canadian Forum. Toronto: New Press 1971.

Quebec: A Chronicle 1968-1972. A Last Post Special. Edited by Nick Auf der Maur and Robert Chodos. With a Postscript by Yvon Charbonneau, Louis Laberge and Marcel Pepin. Toronto: James Lewis & Samuel Publishers 1972.

Report of the Royal Commission on Security (abridged), Ottawa: Information Canada 1969.

SAYWELL, John. *Quebec 70. A Documentary Narrative.* Toronto, Buffalo: University of Toronto Press 1971.

SEGAL, Hugh. *No Surrender: reflections of a happy warrior in the Tory Crusade.* Toronto: HarperCollins Publisher Ltd 1996.

SHACKLETON, Doris French. *Tommy Douglas.* Toronto: McClelland and Stewart 1975.

SMITH, Denis. *Bleeding Hearts...Bleeding Country: Canada and the Quebec Crisis.* Edmonton: M.G. Hurtig LTD Publishers 1971.

STEVENS, Geoffrey. *Stanfield.* Toronto: McClelland and Stewart 1973.

"...Strong and Free...A Response to the War Measures Act", Toronto/ Chicago: New Press 1970.

TARNOPOLSKY, Walter Surma. *The Canadian Bill of Rights,* Second, Revised Edition, Carleton Library No 83. Toronto: McClelland and Stewart Limited 1975.

TETLEY, William. *The October Crisis, 1970. An Insider's View.* Montreal & Kingston, London, Ithaca: McGill-Queen's University Press 2007.

The Asbestos Strike. Joint authorship. Edited by Pierre Elliott Trudeau. Translated by James Boake. Toronto: James Lewis & Samuel 1974.

Tommy Douglas speaks: till power is brought to pooling. Edited by L.D. Lovick. Lantzville B.C.: Oolichan Books 1979.

Touched by Tommy. Edited by Ed and Pemrose Phelan. Regina: WP Phelan Publications 1990.

Towards a Just Society: the Trudeau years. Edited by Tom Axworthy and Pierre Elliott Trudeau. Markham, Ontario; New York, New York: Viking 1990.

Trudeau, Margaret. *Beyond Reason*. New York: Paddington Press: distributed by Grosset & Dunlap 1979.

Trudeau's Shadow. The Life and Legacy of Pierre Elliott Trudeau. Edited by Andrew Cohen and J.L. Granatstein. Toronto: Random House of Canada 1998.

Periodicals

ATWOOD, Margaret. "Untitled," *Saturday Night*, March 1971, p. 8.

Auf der Maur, Nick. "Memoirs of a prisoner of war." *The Last Post*, Vol. 1, No. 5, p. 15.

CANADIAN BAR ASSOCIATION. "Report of Committee on Civil Liberties," *Canadian Bar Review*, 1944, Vol. XXII.

CRUICKSHANK, John. "The 4 am knock on the door," *The Gazette*, October 4, 1980.

DELANEY, Marshall. "Canada's trauma produces a major work of art," *Saturday Night*, June 1975.

FULFORD, Robert. "Against the War Measures," *Saturday Night*, December 1970.

MacPHERSON, Don. "October 1970: People weren't told truth," *The Gazette*, March 16, 1988.

PROCOPE, Mervyn. "October 1970: War Measures," *Canadian Forum*, March 1974, p. 14.

"Profs petition against War Measures Act." *The Varsity*, March 3, 1971.

REILLY, Peter. "The day the Uglies took over politics." *Saturday Night*, December 1970, p. 15.

SMILEY, Donald. "Consent, coercion and confederation," in *Power Corrupted: The October Crisis and The Repression of Quebec,"* edited by Abraham Rotstein for The Canadian Forum. Toronto: New Press 1971.

"Trudeau denounces separatism to U.S. Congress." *Reports on Separatism*, Vol. I, No. 5, Feb. 16 to Feb. 28, 1977.

TRUDEAU, Pierre Elliott. "Lettre de Londres. Réflexions sur une démocratie et sa variante," in *Notre Temps: Hebdomadaire social et culturel*. Vol. III, No. 18, February 14, 1948, pp. 78-82.

WHITAKER, Reg. "Apprehended Insurrection? RCMP Intelligence and the October Crisis," *Queen's Quarterly*, Summer 1993.

ACKNOWLEDGEMENTS

Trudeau's Darkest Hour is an anthology. It exists because of the many authors included and because they, their heirs or publishers graciously agreed to the reproduction of their texts. We thank them very much and at the same time salute the courage of those who, during or after that "doleful October," were not afraid to go against the current.

This book also exists thanks to our friend and publisher, Robin Philpot, who enthusiastically welcomed the idea of doing a book on October 1970 and supported us throughout. He also translated the introduction, the conclusion, and the editors' notes, originally written in French. We sincerely thank him.

Guy BOUTHILLIER and Édouard CLOUTIER

Grateful acknowledgement is made to the following for permission to reprint previously published material.

Margaret Atwood for the right to print her poem Untitled that originally appeared in March 1971 in *Saturday Night* magazine.

Thomas R. Berger for the passages in Chapter 1 and in Chapter 8 taken from *Fragile Freedoms, Human Rights and Dissent in Canada*, Clarke, Irwin, 1981.

John Conway for the passages in Chapter 6 taken from his book *Debts to Pay, The Future of Federalism in Quebec* (third edition, 2004, previously, *Debts to Pay, English Canada from the Conquest to the Referendum*, first edition, 1992).

Robert Fulford for both his review in Chapter 6 of the film *Les ordres* and the article in Chapter 7 first published in *Saturday Night* in December 1970.

Thomas E. Kierans for the excerpt "Our common sense went out the window" from his father Eric Kierans' *Remembering*, Stoddart, 2001.

Terry Mosher (Aislin) for the cartoon first published in *Le Magazine Maclean*, but also published in *The Last Post*.

Hugh Segal for the passage in Chapter 8 from his book *No Surrender: Reflection of a happy warrior in the Tory crusade*, Harper Collins, 1996.

Reg Whitaker for the excerpt in Chapter 5 reprinted from the summer 1993 issue of *Queen's Quarterly*.

Breakwater Books Ltd. for the excerpt in Chapter 4 by Don Jamieson Reprinted from *A World Unto Itself: The Political Memoirs of Don Jamieson* edited by Carmelita McGrath (Breakwater Books, 1989) by permission of the publisher.

James Lorimer & Company Limited for the excerpt in Chapter 8 by Robert Stanfield, reprinted from the introduction to *Rumours of War* by R. Haggart and Aubrey Golden, Lorimer, 1979.

McClelland & Stewart Ltd. and Peter C. Newman for the excerpt in Chapter 5 taken from *Here Be Dragons: Telling Tales of People, Passion and Power*. Used with permission of the publisher.

McClelland & Stewart Ltd. and Desmond Morton for the excerpt in Chapter 8 from *A Military History of Canada: From Champlain to Kosovo* by Desmond Morton. Copyright © 1999 by Desmond Morton. First published in 1985 Hurtig Publishers. Used with permission of the publisher and the author.

McGill-Queen's University Press for the excerpt in Chapter 8 from Ramsay Cook's *The teeth of time, Remembering Pierre Elliott Trudeau*, MQUP 2006.

Random House Canada for the excerpt by Jack Granatstein in Chapter 6 from *Trudeau's Shadow, The Life and Legacy of Pierre Elliott Trudeau* by Andrew Cohen and Jack Granatstein, 1999.

Publisher's note: Despite repeated efforts, the editors and the publisher were unable to reach three authors or their heirs or publishers: Dan G. Loomis for permission to reprint the passage in Chapter 5 from his book *Not Much Glory, Quelling the FLQ* published by Deneau in 1984; the late Nick Auf der Maur's heirs for permission to reprint the article in Chapter 6 from *The Last Post*, November 1970; and Mervyn Procope for permission to reprint the poem in Chapter 6 entitled *October 1970: War Measures* first published in the *Canadian Forum* in 1974. The people concerned are invited to contact the publisher.

Recycled
Supporting responsible use
of forest resources
www.fsc.org Cert no. SGS-COC-003153
© 1996 Forest Stewardship Council

MARQUIS
Marquis Book Printing Inc.

Québec, Canada
2010

Printed on Silva Enviro 100% post-consumer EcoLogo certified paper,
processed chlorine free and manufactured using biogas energy.